RAF CANBERRA UNITS OF THE COLD WAR

£ 4 - 50
FRA
23/12

SERIES EDITOR: TONY HOLMES

OSPREY COMBAT AIRCRAFT 105

RAF CANBERRA UNITS OF THE COLD WAR

ANDREW BROOKES

OSPREY
PUBLISHING

Front Cover

On 3 November 1956, at the height of Operation *Musketeer* (the Suez campaign), No 139 Sqn was tasked with marking Luxor airfield for the main bomber force. The squadron CO, Wg Cdr Paul Mallorie, was flying Canberra B 6 WT370, and his marker aircraft carried a mixed load of Target Indicators (TIs) and 1000-lb bombs, which were proximity fused. He subsequently recalled;

'Having dive-bombed with TIs at last light, we were then supposed to see the raid through and add our contribution of straight-and-level attacks with "thousand pounders". By that time the gyros had completely toppled, the navigators were confused and the bombsights useless. So we made dive-bomb attacks on the parked Il-28 "Beagles" that were there, dropping high explosives.'

WT370 is shown here with the No 139 Sqn flash on the fin and 'Suez stripes' added to reduce friendly fire incidents. On Canberras committed to *Musketeer,* the yellow/black/yellow/black/yellow stripes painted just in front of the tail empennage and from front to back around both the upper and lower surfaces of the wings were two feet wide.

WT370, which had been delivered to the RAF in December 1954, initially served with No 617 Sqn prior to being assigned to No 139 Sqn on the eve of *Musketeer.* Subsequently passed on to No 249 Sqn, the aircraft was converted into a B 15 and issued to Malaya-based No 45 Sqn in late 1962. It was written off in an accident near the unit's base at Kuantan on 23 September 1964. The jet overshot into a rubber plantation after the pilot experienced power loss on landing and missed his approach. Although WT370 was burnt out in the accident, both the pilot (Flg Off P H Sykes) and navigator (Flg Off C G Jefford, who later became a noted aviation historian) were not seriously injured (*Cover artwork by Gareth Hector*)

For Muriel and Nancy

First published in Great Britain in 2014 by Osprey Publishing
PO Box 883, Oxford, OX1 9PL, UK
PO Box 3985, New York, NY 10185-3985, USA

E-mail: info@ospreypublishing.com

Osprey Publishing is part of the Osprey Group

A CIP catalogue record for this book is available from the British Library

ISBN: 978 1 78200 411 0
PDF e-book ISBN: 978 1 78200 412 7
ePub ISBN: 978 1 78200 413 4

Edited by Tony Holmes
Cover Artwork by Gareth Hector
Aircraft Profiles by Chris Davey
Index by Sandra Shotter
Originated by PDQ Digital Media Solutions, UK
Printed in China through Asia Pacific Offset Limited

14 15 16 17 18   10 9 8 7 6 5 4 3 2 1

Osprey Publishing is supporting the Woodland Trust, the UK's leading woodland conservation charity, by funding the dedication of trees.

www.ospreypublishing.com

Acknowledgements
This book could not have been written without the assistance of the Canberra 'old and bold' who gave so unstintingly of their time and patience. Particular thanks must go to Peter Green and Andy Thomas for all their friendship and help with the illustrations.

CONTENTS

IN THE BEGINNING

O n 1 March 1943, more than 250 four-engined RAF bombers dropped 600 tons of bombs on Berlin. Following the raid 500 large fires raged out of control, 20,000 homes were damaged, 35,000 people were rendered homeless and 700 civilians were killed. The following day, a photo-reconnaissance Mosquito circled high over Hitler's capital taking damage assessment photographs in broad daylight. Neither German fighters nor flak could touch it.

The versatile de Havilland Mosquito was designed to operate higher and faster than the opposing air defences. In Lancashire, the company known as English Electric (EE) could only gaze in wonder at the de Havilland creation. In 1938, as part of the huge re-equipment programme for the RAF, EE's Preston factory received contracts to build the Handley Page Hampden medium bomber. After 1941 the Preston facility turned out 2145 Halifax bombers, while also building a flight test airfield at Samlesbury, a few miles away.

In 1944, the company decided to stay in the aircraft business when the war finally ended, but to do that it needed to establish a design team of its own, rather than make other people's aircraft. To lead that team, EE took on William Edward Willoughby Petter, who had been Technical Director/Chief Designer at Westland Aircraft. 'Teddy' Petter designed the Lysander, the Whirlwind and the high-altitude Welkin interceptor, and by mid-1944 he had conceived the basic design for a jet fighter-bomber to replace the Mosquito. This large aircraft was to carry a variety of weapons internally, and various gun installations were proposed, but Westland's directors preferred to concentrate on the lower risk Wyvern propeller-driven strike fighter for the Fleet Air Arm. The disgruntled Petter duly moved to EE as its Chief Engineer of the Aircraft Division at Preston in July 1944.

The first task facing 35-year-old Petter was the recruitment of like minds to his design team – his first appointment, in March 1945, was 'Freddie' Page. The team's home was the spacious showroom of former car dealer Barton Motors, and it was here that Petter and Page prepared a brochure in May 1945 outlining their ideas for a new jet bomber based on the embryonic Westland concept. The fixed internal guns that were originally a feature of the design had by then been deleted.

Staff were quickly recruited to work up a high-speed, high-altitude jet bomber to Specification E 3/45. Petter had originally envisaged an aircraft powered by one large centrifugal compressor 12,000-lb-thrust Nene engine in the centre fuselage. However, once he and Page heard that Rolls-Royce was considering production of the more compact axial-flow AJ 65 (later to become the Avon) engine, the layout was modified to fit one of these in each wing root, leaving the fuselage clear for increased fuel and weapons load.

In July 1945 the EE team concluded that swept wings were not 'yet considered essential or desirable'. A low-aspect ratio wing was chosen instead, which was to give maximum fuel economy at the highest possible

Canberra 'leading lights' at Warton in May 1949. These individuals are, from left to right, Don Crowe (chief structure designer), Dai Ellis (chief aerodynamicist), 'Harry' Harrison (chief draughtsman), A Ellison (chief designer), 'Teddy' Petter (chief engineer), 'Bea' Beamont (chief experimental test pilot), D Smith, Freddy Page (chief stressman) and H Howatt (*Peter Green Collection*)

cruising altitude and to bestow a remarkable manoeuvrability on the bomber. As the design was further refined, the aircraft's engines were moved out of the wing roots and placed in separate wing nacelles. Thereafter, it was a tribute to Petter and his team that the overall layout remained unchanged for the rest of the aircraft's life.

On 7 January 1946 a contract was issued to build four prototypes of what was then known as the English Electric A 1, and shortly thereafter the experimental designation was changed to Spec B 3/45. The RAF's basic A 1 bomber requirement was for a still air range of 1400 nautical miles at a cruising speed of Mach 0.75 at 45,000 ft with 6000 lbs of bombs. These were no small challenges in 1946, and as Samlesbury airfield was unsuitable for projected experimental work, the former USAAF wartime maintenance base at Warton, some five miles west down the Ribble Estuary, was adapted as a flight test centre. World War 2 fighter ace Roland 'Bea' Beamont was taken on as chief experimental test pilot in May 1947.

Tests of A 1 models were carried out in the new wind tunnel at Warton, and in early 1949 assemblies for the first A 1, VN799, began to arrive at the airfield. Reality, however, was now setting in for EE. Spec B 3/45 had called for a 'blind bomber to be laid out for bomb-aiming by radar and other mechanical vision systems'. This referred to the large H2S Mk 9 navigation and bombing radar projected for the V-bombers that was also expected to fit into the lower part of the A 1's nose. But the H2S navigation and bombing radar was becoming so large and complicated, not to mention delayed, that in July 1949 it was announced that 'the Air Staff will not require production of the English Electric blind bomber'.

After a meeting at HQ Bomber Command in late January 1951, Air Chief Marshal (ACM) Sir Ralph Cochrane told the Chief of the Air Staff (CAS) that 'it was generally accepted that the Canberra is a short-range tactical bomber, that there is no equipment which will enable it to hit a small target from 45,000 ft and that it must therefore come down to a height from which it can achieve results'. Consequently, the radar bombing system was replaced with a visual bombsight in the nose, together with an updated wartime Gee-H Mk II navigation system. A third crewmember was added to operate the revised fit, resulting in the specification being updated to B 5/47. The four prototypes retained the 'blind bomber' nose.

The first A 1 VN799, painted in 'Petter' blue overall, was rolled out for engine runs on 2 May 1949. Taxi trials started five days later, and 'Bea' (he disliked the name Roly) got VN799 airborne on 9 May for a short 'hop' to check unstick speed and low-speed control feel. A few more hops followed before, on Friday 13 May, 'Bea' lifted VN799 off for a 30-minute flight. After landing he recorded succinctly in his logbook, 'Satisfactory,

overbalanced rudder'. Before the second flight the top of the rudder was cut down, altering the fully rounded tip to a more flattened line. This shape featured on all subsequent aircraft.

By the end of May Beamont had made ten flights, totalling just over 12 hours. 'Freddie' Page later wrote, 'thus started one of the most straightforward and successful flight test programmes in post-war history'. An altitude of 42,000 ft was reached on 11 August, with Mach 0.80 being achieved the following day. On 31 August the initial design speed of 470 knots was flown at 4500 ft, giving the required margin of 20 knots over the proposed initial service limit of 450 knots indicated air speed (IAS). As Beamont recalled;

'We took that aeroplane to Farnborough in September 1949, and by that time I realised we had a bomber here that could do all the manoeuvres that a fighter could, and more. In some aspects we could actually out-manoeuvre the jet fighters of the day, and we were damn near as fast as the fastest of them. So we broke into the Farnborough display scene with a display that I had worked out privately. The crowd saw this bright blue painted, twin-engined bomber tearing around the airfield, inside the perimeter track, in vertical banked turns, pulling up into rolls off loops and coming down the runway doing rolls like a fighter. They were absolutely astonished.'

Full rolls, roll-off loops and full loops in the A 1 were found to be smooth and straightforward, although some muscle power was required above 350 knots. In its first assessment of VN799, the Aircraft and Armament Experimental Establishment at Boscombe Down assessed the jet as 'extremely satisfactory'.

Up to now it had been policy to name RAF bombers after 'an inland town of the British Commonwealth or associated with British history'. By 1949 Australia was interested in acquiring the new aircraft, and the EE Chairman, Sir George Nelson, proposed that the A 1 should be given the proper name of 'Canberra'. Officialdom agreed and the first four prototypes became Canberra B 1s, to be followed by the operational three-crew B 2. The main difference between the latter machine and the B 1 was the visual bomb-aiming station through the glazed nose, while fitment of the RA 3 engine added 500 lbs of thrust.

That same year 'Teddy' Petter, father of the Lightning supersonic interceptor as well as the Canberra, fell out with the EE hierarchy and

The first English Electric A 1, VN799, finished in 'Petter' blue shortly before its maiden flight on 9 May 1949 (*Peter Green Collection*)

stomped off to design the Gnat for Folland. 'Freddie' Page became the new Chief Engineer, and he was to oversee the Canberra through its varied career for the next 20 years.

NEW B 2

The first B 2 prototype, VX165, made a 45-minute first flight on 21 April 1950. As described in Spec B 5/47;

'The aircraft is a midwing monoplane powered by engines mounted in the wings, carrying a crew of three who are provided with means for ejection. The fuselage is stressed skin of semi-monocoque construction, the nose portion being pressurised with hot/cold control. The upper centre fuselage holds fuel tanks 1, 2 and 3, the lower part being the bomb compartment enclosed by hydraulically retractable doors. The tail portion is of a standard pattern with variable incidence tailplane. Provision is made for a 300-gal long-range tank in the bomb-bay and jettisonable 250-gal tanks are carried on the wingtips. Refuelling of all tanks is by ordinary ground methods, through large orifices.'

The bulk of the Canberra family were to be B 2s or derivatives thereof. The first variant was the photo-reconnaissance version, to Spec PR 31/46, and the prototype PR 3, VX181, flew at Samlesbury on 19 March 1951. Some 36 PR 3s were built, and each one incorporated a 14-in extension to the fuselage forward of the wing to accommodate an extra fuel tank. The centre fuselage could carry up to six day/night cameras, while the rear fuselage had provision for one survey camera and up to 3000 lbs of flares. The overall range was much increased by the addition of 543 gallons of fuel over the B 2, and only a pilot and navigator were carried.

The Canberra T 4, built to Spec T 2/49, was designed for dual-control pilot training. The aim was to replicate the B 2 as closely as possible so the checking pilot was squeezed in via a complex sliding ejection seat arrangement. The T 4 was not required for bombing training so the normal loaded weight was some 7000 lbs less than the B 2, which made for good performance. The prototype T 4, VM467, flew from Samlesbury on 12 June 1952.

With the warming up of the Cold War and growing concerns about the inadequacies of the Mosquitoes and Lincolns of Bomber Command, in March 1949 a production order was given for 90 Canberra B 2s, 34 PR 3s and eight T 4s. The fourth and last B 1 prototype, VN850 with Avon RA 2 engines, reached 50,000 ft on 16 January 1950 and became the first Canberra to attain 500 knots IAS while flashing past Blackpool Tower on 31 July. Ultimately, VX165, the prototype B 2 with Avon RA 3 engines of 6500 lbs thrust, reached 54,500 ft in the hands of 'Bea' Beamont and flight test engineer Dave Walker.

At one stage there was to have been a B 5 variant, intended for the low-level target-marking role with a bomb-aiming radar in the nose and integral wing fuel tanks providing an additional 900 gallons. The solitary prototype B 5, VX185, first flew on 6 July 1951, and its Avon A 7 engines pushed out 7500 lbs thrust each. VX185 carried out the first double Atlantic crossing in one day on 26 August 1952, but no B 5s were ordered into production.

The Korean War stimulated rearmament in the shape of a second order for 143 B 2s, 35 PR 3s and 37 T 4s. Production orders for Canberra B 2s

were placed with Handley Page, Avro, Short Brothers and Harland, as well as EE, in part to keep workforces employed until the V-bombers could enter production, but also to maintain employment in Northern Ireland.

The official Canberra naming ceremony took place at Biggin Hill on 19 January 1951, with the Australian Prime Minister breaking a bottle of champagne over the nose of the first production B 2, WD929. Further Canberra orders were placed early in 1951, but as the nation could ill afford this extravagance while developing three V-bombers, all the 1951 production orders were to be cancelled or modified before manufacture began.

The first production Canberra B 2 for the RAF, WD936, was delivered by 'Bea' Beamont to Binbrook, on the Lincolnshire Wolds, on 25 May 1951. 'Today has been a day of note for Bomber Command', recorded the No 101 Sqn Operational Record Book (ORB), as 'this squadron has received the first of the Command's jet bombers'. Officer Commanding (OC) Binbrook, Gp Capt Wally Sheen, insisted on trying the Canberra for himself before lunch, with Beamont talking him through the flight from the jump seat. That was how things had been done in Bomber Command during World War 2 – 'here are the Pilot's Notes, get on with it' – but compared to the Lincoln, the Canberra flew at almost twice the speed and could operate 20,000 ft higher. Bomber Command was about to enter a whole new era.

Australian Prime Minister Robert Menzies officially names the Canberra at Biggin Hill on 19 January 1951 (*Peter Green Collection*)

'Bea' Beamont (left) poses with Wally Sheen (Station Commander) and Pat Connolly (OC Flying) after delivering the RAF's first production Canberra B 2 to Binbrook on 25 May 1951. WD936 is painted in Bomber Command colours of the period, namely black undersurfaces and light grey uppersurfaces (*Peter Green Collection*)

BINBROOK AND BEYOND

The Bomber Command Jet Conversion Flight, commanded by Flt Lt Bill Morley and two other jet qualified flying instructors, formed at RAF Binbrook during December 1950 with two Meteor T 7 two-seat trainers and two Meteor F 3 single-seaters to give jet experience to those who had only flown piston-engined aircraft up to then. As an Air Ministry report for the first quarter of 1951 put it, 'the first Bomber Command pilots detailed for Canberra conversion have been trained in the techniques of high-altitude, high-speed jet flying. When the Canberra re-equipment programme commences, the Jet Flight will be responsible for the conversion of the squadrons concerned onto the Canberra'.

John Brownlow was a navigator flying Lincolns with No 12 Sqn at Binbrook in 1950;

'I was deputed, together with Flt Lt R A G Barlow of No 101 Sqn, to fly with our Wing Commander Flying, Hamish Mahaddie, a highly decorated Pathfinder pilot. "Rags" Barlow was an experienced wartime navigator while I was the junior boy in the crew. Flying with Hamish eventually led to "Rags" and I becoming members of the first station-level Canberra crew. Hamish always led from the front, so he and Ernest Cassidy were the first station pilots to convert. "Rags" Barlow and I joined them as the first navigator/bomb-aimers then serving in operational squadrons to train as Canberra aircrew.'

At that time Binbrook was one of six heavy-bomber stations in Bomber Command, and it hosted four Lincoln squadrons – Nos 9, 12, 101

Canberra B 2 WD951 is flanked by Meteor T 7s and F 4s of the Jet Conversion Flight at Binbrook in December 1951 (*Peter Green Collection*)

and 617. The three other Lincoln bases were Hemswell (Nos 83 and 97 Sqns), Waddington (Nos 61 and 100 Sqns) and Upwood (Nos 7, 49, 148 and 214 Sqns). The heavy brigade was completed by two Washington B 1 stations – Coningsby (Nos 15, 44 and 149 Sqns) and Marham (Nos 57, 90 and 115 Sqns). The first four Canberra squadrons were to be formed from the Lincoln units at Binbrook, which would become the fount of RAF Canberra knowledge and experience in much the same way as Gaydon subsequently would be for Valiants and Victors.

On 5 July 1951 WD938 suffered the first RAF Canberra accident. After an electrical power failure during a practice overshoot, resulting in the loss of both engines, Flt Lt Thomas managed to make a wheels-up landing on the airfield and neither he nor Ernest Cassidy, who was instructing him, nor the navigator, Sgt Dix, were injured – WD938 flew again on 24 July. No 101 Sqn relinquished its last Lincoln during the course of that same month, but monthly Canberra B 2 production amounted to only one or two airframes in the first half of the year, rising to six in December. Authorised to have ten B 2s, No 101 Sqn had only nine by the end of the year, at which point it was still the only Canberra unit in Bomber Command. Many early Canberras were allocated to experimental flying but 1952 saw a rapid increase in the size of the force to eight (seven bomber and one PR) squadrons.

No 101 Sqn not only absorbed the first operational Canberra crews but it was also made responsible for Canberra Intensive Flying Trials (IFT), which covered the complete operational range and performance of the aircraft together with testing a completely new range of flying clothing. Once the squadron had received its full complement of aircraft and crews, the Air Ministry organised a Press visit to Binbrook, after which *The Aeroplane* reported on 18 January 1952;

'The introduction of the Canberra is more than a re-equipment programme, as it marks the start of the general expansion of Bomber Command. Selected crews from existing Lincolns and Washingtons will convert onto Canberras to form new squadrons, but the piston-engined bombers will remain in service with Bomber Command until the introduction of the Vickers Valiant multi-jet bomber. In the case of No 101 Sqn, commanded by Sqn Ldr Ernest Cassidy DFC, it is flying at two or three times the intensity of normal peacetime squadron routine.

'When an aircraft is in large-scale production, it is preferable that any changes found necessary under intensive operations should be incorporated as soon as possible on the production line, rather than be made retrospectively on a large number of aircraft in general squadron service. IFT should assist

Old and new – Canberra B 2s WD998 and WF907 of No 9 Sqn at Binbrook seen from beneath the wing of a Lincoln B 2 in 1952. The unit commenced its conversion from the Avro piston-engined bomber to the Canberra in May of that year (*Peter Green Collection*)

in accelerating the re-equipment of RAF squadrons with aircraft ready for immediate and effective operational employment.'

Binbrook became the first station in Bomber Command to house four Canberra squadrons – Nos 101, 617, 12 and 9 Sqns – with administration of the Jet Conversion Flight becoming the responsibility of No 617 Sqn until No 231 Operational Conversion Unit (OCU) was established at Bassingbourn on 1 December 1951 to convert crews to the Canberra. After Binbrook, another No 1 Group station, Hemswell, began to exchange its Mosquito B 35s for Canberras. Nos 109 and No 139 Sqns made up the Bomber Command Marker Force, and the former converted on to Canberras in August-September 1952. No 139 Sqn received its first Canberras during November 1952, but because of winter weather it was not until the following February that the ORB was able to record;

'All crews are now converted to Canberras. The general opinion seems to be that the Canberra handles well on instrument approaches and its single-engine performance is exceptionally good.'

Both squadrons subsequently resumed their role as the Light Marker Force in Bomber Command exercises.

A fifth Binbrook squadron – No 50 Sqn – formed during August 1952, with its first Canberra B 2 arriving on the 18th. Thus, by the end of 1952, Bomber Command's Canberra force consisted of five Main Force light bomber squadrons, two marker squadrons and the beginnings of a Canberra PR squadron. Official totals at the end of the year were 70 B 2s authorised and 48 in service, plus eight PR 3s authorised and one delivered. The official return for October-December 1952 reported that 'the five Binbrook and two Hemswell squadrons are now equipped to eight UE (Unit Establishment), and that some of the No 139 Sqn crews are still undergoing conversion training by the Jet Conversion Flight'.

A Canberra policy meeting held on 9 January 1951 was briefed that 'the Canberra B 2 is designed as a short-range day bomber. Owing to its navigation limitations it cannot effectively be operated outside Gee cover except in visual conditions. Its role in Bomber Command has therefore been defined as bombing in support of the land battle within 250 miles of the frontline'. The brief stressed the importance of marking targets that were beyond the range of ground-based aids. 'From high altitudes, target identification makes visual day bombing difficult. For accurate bombing, therefore, there is a continuing need both by day and by night to be able to mark targets accurately. There will, therefore, be a requirement for an aircraft to mark visually for a medium-range Canberra force'. The implication was that, provided the Canberras operated over Europe, where they could use Gee, they could bomb effectively. Outside of Gee cover they needed a marker force.

In John Brownlow's words, 'the only navigation aid, other than VHF bearings and Rebecca, was Gee and an Air Position Indicator. The Gee box was the Universal Indicator, allowing Gee or Gee-H to be selected. At the time, Bomber Command navigators were trained to stick to track and take a Gee fix every six minutes. This basic procedure was no more difficult in a Canberra than in a Lincoln, and generally it was easier to track accurately because of the higher speed and smaller drift angles.

'From the start, navigators were responsible for maintaining the "HOWGOZIT" graph, taking periodic fuel readings and plotting them against planned time, predicted fuel remaining and distance. The published Canberra fuel consumption figures were very accurate, which was just as well as the fuel reserve margins were much lower than those we were accustomed to on the Lincoln.'

Commander-in-Chief (C-in-C) Bomber Command, Air Marshal (AM) Sir Hugh Lloyd, expected to have ten Canberra squadrons by the end of 1952, but in the event he had Nos 101, 617, 12 and 9 (formed in that order) at Binbrook, No 109 at Hemswell and No 50 Sqn at Binbrook in August 1952, No 139 Sqn at Hemswell in November 1952 and the eighth, No 540 PR Sqn at Benson, which received its first PR 3 in December 1952. The RAF was expanding Bomber Command according to under Plan H, which called for Sir Hugh Lloyd to also have ten Lincoln and eight Washington squadrons at his disposal by December 1952.

In a directive from CAS, dated 20 March 1950, the C-in-C had been told, 'Your principal effort is likely to be directed against targets within 250 miles of the Rhine so that full advantage can be taken of maximum bomb-loads and navigational aids to bombing'. Another note from CAS, dated 1 March 1952, on British bomber policy stated that 'the ultimate build-up of the bomber force under Plan H aims at the provision of 560 light bombers and 152 medium bombers. All the light bombers are committed to the support of Supreme Allied Commander Europe (SACEUR) and, in fact, constitute the main part of his striking force'. The primary task of the Canberra force once it had been built up was to help halt a Soviet advance into West Germany.

The terms 'light' and 'medium' conformed with USAF terminology that was based on radius of action rather than all-up-weight – 'light' meant less than 1000 nautical miles and 'medium' 1000-2500 nautical miles. The V-bombers were to be designated the Medium Bomber Force (MBF), while CAS described the Canberra as 'a good modern light bomber for tactical use at night and in bad weather against airfields, communications, etc.' The Chiefs of Staff, in their 12 October 1950 'Report on the Size and Shape of the Armed Forces over the Three Years beginning 1951/52', said that most of Bomber Command's 36 frontline squadrons by the end of 1953/54 would be equipped with the Canberra, 'which can only carry 6000 lbs over a radius of 500 miles, and its hitting power will be small in relation to its commitments in support of the defence of the UK and the land battle in Europe'.

The build-up of the Canberra light bomber force reflected the pledge made by Prime Minister Clement Atlee to the North Atlantic Council in December 1950 'to strengthen the defences of the free world'. CAS (Marshal of the RAF Sir John Slessor) said on 10 March 1952 that the personnel manning the RAF squadrons were 'the only people [apart from the Americans] who could make a serious bomber contribution to NATO'. Because the B-29 Washingtons and Lincoln were obsolescent and the Valiant had not yet flown, 'the only other bet was the Canberra, and we ordered as many of them as we could get to build up a first-line force of 560 in the UK, all for the support of SHAPE (Supreme Headquarters Allied Powers Europe).'

Thus, from its inception, the RAF Canberra Light Bomber Force (LBF) was committed to the defence of Europe – 'The light bomber component of your force will be operated wholly in support of SACEUR, and controlled

Canberra B 2s WD944 and WD934 of No 101 Sqn fly in close formation near Binbrook for the benefit of the camera in December 1951 (*Peter Green Collection*)

by you on his behalf', wrote CAS (ACM Sir William Dickson) to C-in-C Bomber Command (AM Sir George Mills) on 13 May 1953.

Initially, Mills' main force squadrons were based in the UK, and it was not until August 1954 that the first Canberras deployed to Germany, and even then were still operationally controlled by Bomber Command. 'Although the Canberra Light Bomber Force is part of RAF Bomber Command', wrote VCAS to the Defence Minister on 20 January 1956, 'it is wholly assigned to SACEUR except for the Marker Squadrons. The Medium Bomber Force is retained under the control of Her Majesty's Government, but the Minister of Defence agreed on 17 December 1953 that one of its primary tasks in war would be retardation operations designed to assist SACEUR'.

The year 1953 saw the re-equipment of Washington B 1 units with Canberras. No 44 Sqn was the first to start conversion training, followed by Nos 149, 57 and 15 Sqns. At the beginning of the year No 10 Sqn, whose previous existence had been flying Halifax IIIs in the transport role, was re-formed at Scampton. Its ORB recorded that 'the squadron commander, Sqn Ldr Donald "Podge" Howard, was posted in from RAF Binbrook, where he had completed a tour of duty as flight commander on No 101 Sqn. Eight crews, two from RAF Binbrook and six from No 231 OCU, assembled at Scampton'. No 44 Sqn got its first B 2s in April, when it became the first Canberra unit at Coningsby. No 149 Sqn, the second Washington squadron to be converted to Canberras, was not far behind. Two more Washington units then began to re-equip with Canberras, No 57 Sqn receiving its first two B 2s on the 12 May and No 15 Sqn a fortnight later.

By the end of 1953 there were 17 Canberra bomber and three Canberra PR squadrons. Twelve months later, there were 24 squadrons in the UK and three in Germany, the latter being 'under overall policy control of Bomber Command but under day-to-day operational control of 2nd TAF'. The Canberra LBF reached its zenith at the end of April 1955, with 390 aircraft equipping 27 squadrons. The UK had fulfilled the RAF bomber rearmament programme requirements instituted after the North Atlantic Council meeting in December 1950. As the V-bombers that could reach deep into the USSR entered service, they were manned by Canberra men like 'Podge' Howard, who was selected to be the first Vulcan squadron commander. Truly, the Canberra LBF was in the van of jet bomber expertise.

TRAINING DAYS

No 231 OCU's ORB for December 1951 outlined its title as the 'Bomber Command Operational Conversion Unit' and its task as 'training pilots, navigators and radar operators to reinforce PR and light bomber squadrons at home and overseas'. During February No 231 OCU accepted its first two Canberras, and the following month a high aircraft utilisation figure of 89 hr 50 min on the pair was achieved. Canberra familiarisation flying continued during April, with all instructors completing one night solo.

The first No 231 OCU Canberra course, totalling five crews, assembled on 27 May 1952 and passed out on 26 August, by which time there were 21 B 2s at Bassingbourn. The second course (nine crews) passed out on 17 September, and by July 1953 the OCU had 30 Canberra B 2s plus a T 4 trainer, together with ten Meteor T 7 trainers. The flying task hammered the groundcrews who, according to an *Air Clues* article published in 1977, were 'largely National Service and poorly paid, and worked in primitive conditions from unheated, poorly lit and unsanitary dispersal huts. They were under constant pressure to produce serviceable aircraft for the intensive flying effort. Shortage of components and inadequate stock control necessitated frequent "robbing" of items from one aircraft to make another serviceable for the flying programme. Bomb racks were so scarce that if an aircraft became unserviceable before flight, the crew had to wait for a second aircraft to be armed from scratch with the bomb rack from the first'.

When I converted onto the Canberra at No 231 OCU, it was made clear that the early Avon engines had no overspeed governor, and if you opened the throttles too quickly, you risked ending up with a big glider. To illustrate the point, both engines flamed out at 15,000 ft during steep turns on a Bassingbourn B 2 on 11 August 1953. The pilot was unable to relight the engines and the Canberra was force-landed near Debden without injury to its crew. At that time the OCU was flying around 1000 hours a month, and 23 Canberra crews graduated by the end of 1953.

On 22 June 1951, C-in-C Bomber Command thanked CAS 'for your letter of 13 June in which you asked me to consider the two alternatives – i.e. two or three in a crew for a Canberra. I accept the recommendation that we should plan for a crew of two'.

Derek Tuthill joined the RAF in 1951 and trained as a navigator on Wellingtons during the Korean War expansion period. He went to the Command Bombing

No 35 Sqn Canberra B 2s conduct a formation flypast over their Upwood home on 16 June 1959 (*Author*)

Canberra B 2 WD980 of No 617 Sqn flies over the Lincolnshire coast in 1953. This aircraft had been delivered new to the Binbrook-based unit when it switched from Lincoln B 2s to Canberra B 2s in early 1952 (*Peter Green Collection*)

School at Lindholme in the summer of 1953 to practice visual bombing from Lincolns, which were largely flown by Czech and Polish pilots. 'The UK was full of bombing ranges back then – there was an inland range near Lindholme, two in the Suffolk forests and one north of Oxford for starters, not to mention all the coastal ones. We dropped 25-lb practice bombs using a T 2 bombsight in the great big glasshouse that was the Lincoln nose'.

Derek was then posted to Bassingbourn on the Long Bomber Course – the Short Course was for those with jet experience – whereupon his course helped form No 40 Sqn at Coningsby in late October 1953. 'Four months later the squadron moved to Wittering, where we watched No 100 Sqn's Lincolns fly out to be scrapped. We flew with one pilot and one navigator in those days. I did both plotting and bomb aiming, but after a year a third guy was brought in'.

The Canberra emitted a series of pulses that triggered ground beacons to transmit a corresponding series of pulses. The delay between transmission and reception of the transponded pulse from the ground was directly proportional to the range of the aircraft from the beacon. By measuring the distance to the ground station, the bomber was able to navigate along a circular arc in the sky, dropping its bombs when it reached a pre-computed distance from another station. The accuracy of the fix, however, depended on the angle at which the two range vectors intersected, being greatest when they intersected at right angles.

In Derek Tuthill's words, 'we navigated with Gee and used H for bombing. The Canberra was flown round the Gee-H circle. There were two lines on the 12-inch cathode ray tube, one of which was the tracker. The navigator directed the aircraft onto the required track, briefed the pilot on direction of transmitter and final heading, then helped him maintain track by reporting distance off-track as "Too near" (to transmitter) or "Too far" (from transmitter), plus Distance off – "25 yards, 50 yards, 75 yards" or even more.

Canberra B 2 WD980, now with No 15 Sqn, takes off from Honington in September 1955. This aircraft was eventually disposed of at the Catterick Fire School in 1977 (*Peter Green Collection*)

'At the same time the navigator controlled the timing device (the "Mouse"), which calculated bomb release, calling "Bomb Doors Open" at the appropriate time. Provided the bomb release switches had been activated and the bomb doors opened, the system released the ordnance automatically. This was far more accurate than visual bombing, especially from 40,000 ft. Canberra visual bombing was inaccurate compared with that achieved with the Doppler-fed bombsight in the Valiant. In the Canberra, the run to the target required constant correction. In the Valiant, once the target had been located in the bombsight, corrections were rarely required.'

Transmitters in the Canberras operated in the 20-80 megahertz band, and used a pulse recurrence frequency in the neighbourhood of 100 cycles per second. The time taken by the beacon to receive a pulse, send out the response and return to the receiver was about 100 microseconds. With a pulse recurrence frequency of 100 cycles per second, a beacon would be busy for 10,000 microseconds in any one second dealing with the enquiries of one aircraft. It would therefore have 990,000 microseconds free in each second in which to respond to other aircraft, giving a theoretical maximum handling capacity of 100 aircraft. In practice, the aircraft could not be expected to phase their pulses so as to make the best possible use of the beacons and, therefore, a handling capacity of 70 to 80 Canberras was the sensible limit. The basic Gee-H concept remains in use today as the civilian Distance-Measuring Equipment system.

A pulsed navigation system like Gee was relatively easy to jam by simply sending out additional pulses on the same frequency, cluttering up the display and making it very difficult for the operator to read the signal. With Gee-H, each aircraft had its own unique timing and, therefore, there were dozens of such transmitters so the magnitude of the jamming problem became considerably more difficult. Moreover, as the Gee-H system used existing Gee equipment, simply switching off the transmitter turned it back into a normal Gee unit that could be directly read on a map, which made it useful when navigating over northwest Europe in peacetime.

George Worrall completed his navigator training in Winnipeg during 1952-53 and then had his first flights in a Canberra after being temporarily assigned as a 'Safety Observer' to No 15 Sqn at Coningsby. On 11 December 1953, HQ Bomber Command stated that two navigators were to be carried on all details involving the release of practice or live bombs, the second being there 'solely for monitoring purposes'. The high mission workload, together with a series of incidents involving practice bombs falling outside the designated danger areas, led to a pilot and two navigator crews – one nominally the plotter and the other the bomb-aimer who worked Gee – becoming the norm.

On 29 May 1953, *Flight* magazine published the following overview of RAF Bomber Command;

'Three or more squadrons inhabit most bomber stations and answer directly to Group HQ. The first jet Canberra B 2 light bombers now coming into service are not only replacing the old type "heavies" but are equipping newly-formed squadrons as well. A small number of Lincoln and Washington squadrons will remain in service until replaced by Valiants. But Bomber Command is in the process of developing intensively its new procedures and methods, new equipment and new tactics. It is

Canberra B 2 WH640 of No 109 Sqn
was photographed on a damp
flightline at Boscombe Down in
February 1953. The yellow and black
fin flash mirrors the red and black
flash of its sister squadron at
Hemswell, No 139 Sqn. Parked
behind the Canberra are an Avro York
C 1 and an Avro Shackleton MR 2
(*Peter Green Collection*)

finally leaving behind the 20,000 ft, 200 mph era, and changing over to 40,000 or more feet and 500 mph. Sweet-to-handle Canberras provide an ideal introductory step to the four-engined jet bomber.'

Training often culminated in exercises such as *Jungle King*, on which *Flight* staff members got airborne. One reporter was assigned to a Marham-based Washington;

'At 1750 hrs, dead on time, we accelerated rapidly into the air under the influence of 2000 bhp from each Cyclone engine. Navigation was by radar fixes over Germany, and the navigator came up to the nose for the bombing run. We levelled out at 19,600 ft at 180 mph IAS. Navigation had been by radar fixes over Germany, and on the intercom one could hear the "steadies" being given to the captain as the target drew nearer. At 2003 hrs the "bombs" were released. At 2031 hrs the gun turret switches were turned off, and half-an-hour later we again crossed the coast and started our descent at 220 mph. Back in the nose, I was able to listen in to VHF control from Marham tower, and hear the aircraft being "stacked" before landing.'

This trundle over Germany would not have surprised a Lancaster crew operating in 1944, but the same could not have been said about another *Flight* journalist's sortie in a Binbrook Canberra simulating an attack on an airfield at Bremen;

'From the clothing store we drew a selection of new expensive-looking equipment – helmet, mask, pressure waistcoat, flying overalls, gauntlets, suede boots and long woollen stockings. Unfamiliar items are the pressure-fed mask and waistcoat – equipment necessitated by the possibility of pressure-cabin failure above 40,000 ft.

'A "B" form, calling for an attack that evening, had come from Group HQ, and the general briefing of crews was about to begin. The commanding officer, Sqn Ldr J C M Mountford, added a sweater, "Mae West" and woollen mittens to my equipment, and we joined the crew – Sgt Kenneth Neate (pilot) and Flg Off Kenneth Hancock (navigator) – in the briefing room. Maps and flight plans, issued 30 minutes earlier, were already spread out on the briefing-room tables.

'The Canberras' attack would take the form of a shallow penetration routed to avoid the enemy's defences. One by one, briefing officers took their place on the rostrum to issue information, instructions and advice on navigation, radar, bombing, signals, intelligence, meteorology and air traffic control. Speeches were quick and to the point, with crisp interpolations from the commander flying.

'Very soon crews were disembarking from cars, trucks or Land Rovers at various dispersal points, exchanging final words with ground staff and climbing aboard their aircraft. Sole admittance to the Canberra crew-section is by the pressure-sealed door on the right-hand side of the nose. Parallel to the door, but on the left, is the pilot's ejector seat. Similar seats, placed side-by-side, are provided aft for the two navigators. While Sgt Neate began his cockpit checks I attached the dinghy to my "Mae West", buckled up the parachute and seat harness and plugged in the intercom and oxygen leads.

'At 1759 hrs, precisely on schedule, the Canberra accelerated down the runway. By 1800 hrs the cockpit had grown brighter, indicating that we were rapidly leaving behind not only the airfield but also the cloud layer that covered it. Apart from a surprisingly gentle pressure on the back, there was no other sensation. Away in front two brown contrails revealed companions from Binbrook en route for Bremen. We reached our cruising height of some eight miles in less time than it would take to smoke a cigarette. At altitude the Canberra is rock-steady, and only the hiss of air betrays motion through the rarefied atmosphere. We cruised at a constant Mach reading of 0.7+, which, allowing for height and an outside air temperature of -62°C, meant over 500 mph.

Canberra B 2s of No 27 Sqn start their engines whilst parked on the grass dispersal area at Scampton in June 1954, prior to the unit embarking on a European tour to Greece, France, Italy, Portugal and Yugoslavia (*Peter Green Collection*)

Canberra B 2s WH924 and WH922 of No 61 Sqn flank WH741 of No 109 Sqn during a 1955 photo sortie from Hemswell (*Peter Green Collection*)

'Absence of cloud in the target area did not affect our simulated blind-bombing attack. Only 45 minutes had passed since take-off. The crew, concentrating on their instruments to ensure perfect accuracy, could hardly spare a second to glance at the ground – the clear-vision bombing position in the nose remained unoccupied, and Flg Off Hancock continued to direct the pilot from the navigator-plotter's seat. Normally the run over the target is controlled by a third crew member – the observer – who assists with en route navigation.

'Having disposed of our "bomb load", we were able to decrease further the chances of interception by adding 5000 ft to our cruising height. Despite the very impressive figure already shown on the altimeter, the climb was effortless and very quick indeed. By now, condensed moisture in the cabin had frozen and formed a glaze on every metal surface, but the interior remained warm. Air tapped from the Avon compressors kept the cabin "altitude" below 25,000 ft.

'Listening out for a possible order to divert, we turned on the navigation lights and began a rapid descent 50 miles from base. Sgt Neate began the descent at increased Mach number. Dive-brakes were extended, steepening the dive, and we continued to shed height. We pulled out over the cloud blanket covering Spurn Head, the Humber and Grimsby, and flew on at 30,000 ft beyond Binbrook to Lincoln. Above us were contrails, like chalk marks on black velvet, marking the homeward path of other Binbrook Canberras

'Permission to descend and turn into the GCA [ground-controlled approach] pattern was refused, since other aircraft were just taking their place in this part of the landing queue. We orbited once and again called "overhead" – this time our Canberra was accepted and we began a 5000 ft/min descent at a specified Mach number, soon turning onto course for the airfield at the appointed height, for our aircraft, of 17,000 ft. Cloud-base at Binbrook was only 300-400 ft, with visibility of 2000 yards, and the pilot prepared for a GCA. As the Canberra scudded into cloud a few miles from the runway, with dive-brakes extended to reduce speed, the reassuring voice of the controller came through.

'Canberra PR 3s are coming into service to replace the few remaining Mosquitoes. Another Canberra duty is that of conversion to jet bombers – at present undertaken at Bassingbourn. For all this flying, the squadrons depend heavily upon their willing but scarce groundcrews. There are still all-too-few skilled men in Bomber Command, and in particular there is a need for those whose work it is to keep the special navigation and blind-bombing equipment serviceable.

'Battleships and tanks have their place, but it is the jet bombers which will constitute the country's most powerful war-winning force.'

CREW CLASSIFICATION

In a directive dated 4 July 1952, C-in-C Bomber Command told Air Vice Marshal (AVM) Dermot Boyle (Air Officer Commanding No 1 Group) and AVM William Brook (Air Officer Commanding No 3 Group) that he was to be informed of the Command's state of readiness, and that he wanted *all* crews to be classified as Select, Combat or Non-combat with immediate effect. A constituted crew was regarded as a team, and an appendix to the directive stated that Select crews were to hold their classification for six months and they were authorised to land anywhere outside the UK. Combat crews were to hold their classification for four months and could land in the UK and Germany only. Non-combat crews could land only in the UK.

Squadrons with fewer than four Select or Combat crews were to be regarded as non-operational. Select crew captains were to have a current green Instrument Rating and, for Canberra captains, 100 hours on type, of which 50 hours had to be at night. A Crew Classification Scheme issued by HQ Bomber Command on 30 December 1953 outlined the air qualification for Select and Combat bomb-aimers, together with Select and Combat standards for pilots and navigators in low-level marker squadrons.

Derek Tuthill was qualified in both Canberra navigation roles, and to this day he remembers the No 40 Sqn Canberra that he flew the most, WJ727;

'If you were lucky enough to get an English-Electric built aircraft, you guarded that with your life. An Avro-made aircraft was second and those constructed by Handley Page and Shorts were third equal. I did fly other Canberras – you had to when your aircraft went into hangar for servicing, but 80 per cent of my flying was in WJ727.'

Having received its shiny new jet bombers, the RAF was very keen to show them off to the world. On 18 April 1952, Sir Hugh Lloyd flew to the United States in a Canberra, returning on 9 May. On 28 September he went in another Canberra to Nairobi in 9 hr 55 min. But the most impressive 1952 foray overseas was mounted by four B 2s of the newly reformed No 12 Sqn, which left Binbrook on 20 October for a 24,000-mile goodwill tour of South America led by Air Officer Commanding No 1 Group, AVM Dermot Boyle.

Each Exercise *Round Trip* Canberra had a three-man crew, and on the outward flight AVM Boyle set an unofficial record on 23 October of 4 hr 27 min for the South Atlantic crossing from Dakar to Recife. Subsequently, *Flight*'s American correspondent reported that it had been very good for

Canberra B 2s WD987, WD983 and WD996 of No 12 Sqn have been parked alongside Hastings C 2 transports of No 53 Sqn at Binbrook in October 1952 prior to Exercise *Round Trip* to South America. The Canberra was sold to the US Air Force before it entered RAF service, making it the first British military aircraft to be built in America since the DH 4 in 1917. Note that the B 2 closest to the camera has been adorned with an air vice-marshal's 'star plate' immediately beneath the No 12 Sqn lightning bolt. This aircraft was flown throughout *Round Trip* by exercise leader AVM Dermot Boyle, Air Officer Commanding No 1 Group, and his navigator, Flt Lt B Brownlow (*Peter Green Collection*)

British prestige in Latin America. He also made the point that in some of the smaller Central American states, the aircraft were described as being American, the assumption being that only the US made jets. He added that it was not considered necessary to send out any spare Avon engines for the Canberras, and nor did they need any, but it was a pity that this fact was not publicised.

Apart from the prestige factor, such overseas trips were useful in proving the new aircraft over long distances, and giving crews experience of flying and navigating over foreign territory. It was also a test of servicing Canberras away from their home base. Lone Rangers became the norm for Canberra crews, and George Worrall got as far as Nairobi in a No 18 Sqn jet. Derek Tuthill recalls that for long-distance navigation, 'we had Gee and Rebecca but no Radio Compass. We flew Lone Rangers as far as Aden, via Idris in Libya and Khartoum in Sudan. There was a technique in flying the Idris-Khartoum leg. You could get a true bearing from Idris out to 100 miles, but that was that. So you deliberately aimed left till you saw the Nile and flew down to Khartoum from there. It was a bit hit and miss but it worked. Between Khartoum and Aden, you got plenty of true bearings courtesy of International Aeradio stations. I think they were paid for each true bearing they transmitted, and when they heard a RAF jet coming through, they knew they would get their money'.

'Fitted with wingtip drop tanks', wrote George Worrall, 'the range of the Canberra B 2 was just sufficient to reach the Soviet satellite countries of the Warsaw Pact. At the time, the aircraft was the mainstay of the RAF bomber force, with its trained crews aimed at discouraging any ambitions the Soviets may have in threatening the integrity of either us or our allies. Most mass exercises were designed to reflect this, but normal training was dedicated to improving crew skills. For navigators this meant navigation and bombing exercises by day and night using all means at our disposal – radio aids, visual, astro-navigation and, of course, mental dead reckoning.

'For me and many others, the most remarkable feature of the Canberra was its service ceiling. Cruise climb profiles might see us getting just above 48,000 ft, although the jet's performance began to decline sharply above 45,000 ft. We regularly operated above 40,000 ft, and a Select crew was cleared to visually bomb a practice target from 45,000 ft.'

The Canberra B 2 carried six 1000-lb iron bombs on Avro triple carriers – Canberras would not be armed with nuclear weapons until 1958. 'We did no target study as they would do on the V-force', recalled Derek Tuthill. 'The hierarchy was never specific on targets. We just had the capability to deliver 1000-lb bombs as accurately as we could from 40,000 ft, although we practised dropping from much lower altitudes'.

The extent to which British aerial thinking was still rooted in World War 2 was illustrated by Exercise *Dividend* flown in July 1954. Some 6000 sorties were generated by RAF, Fleet Air Arm and USAF attackers against the UK, with four major night raids coming in over the North Sea at heights between 30,000 ft and 50,000 ft. 'We attacked on a broad front', recalled Derek Tuthill. 'The simulated drop line ran diagonally up the east coast from Manston in Kent (51.20N) to Leuchars in Fife (56.22N). Along that line, there was a Canberra every mile. After the "attack", you could switch your navigation lights back on.'

John Brownlow began pilot conversion training in April 1953, and 19 months later he joined No 103 Sqn, one of the four Canberra B 2 units of No 551 Wing at Gütersloh in Germany;

'This wing was really an extension of Bomber Command in terms of policy direction and, hence, concept of operations. We used Gee-H Mk 2 for blind bombing and the T2 bombsight for visual bombing, as we had done from the outset. The main focus was on Gee-H, dropping 25-lb practice bombs, usually on Nordhorn Range. A most significant operational limitation of Gee-H was that it covered the UK and Europe only up to a line – roughly Rostock-Magdeburg-Munich. Strategic operational control of the wing was retained by HQ Bomber Command, but day-to-day control of routine flying and administration was devolved to 2nd Tactical Air Force [TAF] via HQ No 2 Group. For exercise and operational planning purposes we were integrated with Bomber Command Canberra wings, and we used the same aircrew classification system.'

With its amiable aerodynamics and docile flying characteristics, the Canberra was a well-liked aircraft. Derek Tuthill was the plotter on the No 49 Sqn Valiant that dropped the first real British hydrogen bomb southeast of Christmas Island in the Pacific on 8 November 1958. Known as *Grapple 'X'*, the two-stage thermonuclear bomb exploded with a force of 1.8 MT at around 8000 ft. Back up at 45,000 ft, 'We just waited for the shock-wave, which came some two-and-a-half minutes after weapon release. It was definitely noticeable, but a non-event compared with rolling a Canberra!'

However, early Canberras suffered from 'runaway' tailplane electrical trim actuator problems. The first incident of this kind occurred on 26 July 1953, and subsequently there were 50 reports of serious actuator faults, 14 of them resulting from runaway tail trim. In one No 231 OCU B 2 incident on 26 September 1955, three of the four crew members survived after the tailplane actuator moved to the fully nose-up position and the aircraft become uncontrollable. By rolling it into a steep turn the instructor

Canberra B 2 WH914 of No 100 Sqn is bombed up at Wittering in October 1955. Delivered new to the unit soon after the squadron replaced its Lincoln B 2s with Canberra B 2s from April 1954, this aircraft subsequently served with Nos 61, 50, 76 and 35 Sqns, before finishing its RAF career with No 231 OCU. Sold to BAE in October 1981, it was converted into a B 92 for the Argentine Air Force but not delivered because of the Falklands War. Put into storage, the bomber was scrapped at Samlesbury in 1988 (*Peter Green Collection*)

'regained partial control until the two navigators had ejected and the student pilot had escaped through the entrance hatch. He then made a safe ejection himself, but was slightly injured during the descent when his parachute became tangled with the ejection seat. Although the student navigator's body was found still strapped into his seat, the remaining two crew members landed without injury'.

A runaway tailplane actuator would cause the aircraft to go into an irreversible steep climb or dive. Following seven incidents on B 2s, five of which were fatal, all Canberras with single-speed actuators were grounded. The fault was eventually traced to mechanical 'sticking-on' of the single pole trim switch, which caused the actuator to run out to full travel after the pilot had released the switch. The 'fix' was to progressively retrofit all marks of Canberra with a new dipole duplicate trim switch, improved wiring integrity and revised actuator stops to reduce overall travel.

There were also problems with 'freezing' ailerons and stress corrosion in the new DTD 683 aluminium alloy, but these were all sorted out and, in 'Bea' Beamont's words, 'subsequent production testing of all Canberra variants was straightforward, lacking in severe complication and generally described by those involved as "no bother at all"'.

The Canberra was manoeuvrable enough for a formation aerobatic team to be formed in 1956 with four aircraft, but the limitations of the navigation and bombing equipment confined B 2s to tactical battlefield-support in Europe. Fast, high altitude Canberras would have survived much better than the Blenheims and Battles of 1940, but those at the top of the RAF were under no illusions about the efficacy of the strike effect. Back in September 1951, VCAS wrote to ACAS (OR) to say, 'My own feelings are that Gee-H has surprised us by the accuracy which can be achieved now that crews know how to use the set, but that the serviceability is bad and will never be good. We must seriously consider how quickly we can replace it with better equipment'. Such limitations of the Canberra force were bought into particularly sharp focus when it was suddenly sent out to take part in the Suez campaign.

PHOTOGRAPHIC MEMORIES

In October 1950, a Strategic Photo-Reconnaissance conference was held at Benson, in Oxfordshire, with the cover for the event programme featuring a reconnaissance aircraft peeling back the Iron Curtain. In his opening remarks, Assistant Chief of Air Staff (Intelligence), Gp Capt Gerard Paul, regretted that 'we have virtually no photo-intelligence of the enemy at present'. He noted that Soviet anti-aircraft systems could be lethal up to 46,000 ft, and what was needed was a PR aircraft that could fly at 50,000 ft and above, equipped with good 48-in focal length lenses, and eventually a panoramic camera fit for maximum area coverage.

As if in answer to Gp Capt Paul's prayer, the Canberra PR 3 made its first flight six months before the Benson conference. Although capable of reaching above 50,000 ft, long-range navigation was a problem pending availability of the first Green Satin Doppler radar navigation system after 1954-55. As it happened, the 14-in extension to the PR 3 fuselage, coupled with redistributed mass, resulted in excessive vibration that delayed the PR 3's entry into operational service. It was not until December 1952 that No 540(PR) Sqn, hitherto equipped with Mosquito PR 34As, received the first production PR 3, WE135, at Benson. The squadron ORB for that month recorded that 'the first Canberra PR Mk 3 is not equipped with the necessary mountings for cameras, so photographic trials cannot yet be carried out. However, aircrew and groundcrew conversion and familiarisation are proceeding'.

The introduction of the Canberra PR 3 into RAF service was followed by development of the Canberra PR 7 with Avon RA 7 engines, wing leading edge fuel tanks and Maxaret anti-skid brakes. As if to proclaim its capability, the first PR 7, WH773, was entered in the England-New Zealand Air Race of October 1953 in concert with two PR 3s. In the words of one PR nav, 'it was set up for Wg Cdr Lewis "Bob" Hodges from HQ Bomber Command to win the race'. However, although WH773 covered the 5416 miles between London and Colombo, Ceylon, in 10 hr 25 min 21 sec (at an average speed of 519.5 mph), and flew non-stop from Colombo to Perth (omitting the Cocos Islands), WH773 then went unserviceable with generator and filler-cap trouble, resulting in Hodges and his navigator, Sqn Ldr R Currie, only coming fourth.

To the great delight of many at crew-room level, 'the Air Race was won by a couple of PR mates, Flt Lts Roland "Monty" Burton and Don Gannon, flying PR 3 WE139'. Some 10,000 New Zealanders, including their Prime Minister, waited in torrential rain at Christchurch to greet Burton and Gannon as they crossed the finishing line some 23 hr 51 min 7 sec after leaving London Airport – a record that still stands today.

The sixth production Canberra PR 3 WE140 of No 540 Sqn was photographed at Heathrow airport. The unit, hitherto equipped with Mosquito PR 34As, had received the first production PR 3s at Benson from December 1951. WE140 subsequently spent much of its service career with Nos 231 and 237 OCUs (*Author*)

Throughout the journey, when WE139 spent just 90 minutes on the ground, the two men never left the aircraft while RAF personnel, who had been pre-positioned at each of the four refuelling stops, serviced the PR 3. Burton and Gannon were each awarded the Air Force Cross upon their return to the UK.

A year earlier, RAF Bomber Command experienced high-level jet operations when a Special Duties Flight was formed at Sculthorpe, in Norfolk, with three ex-USAF North American RB-45C Tornadoes. The offer to loan them to the RAF had been made by Gen Hoyt S Vandenberg, USAF Chief of Staff, in early 1951, and the flights made in them on 17-18 April and 12-13 December 1952 were the fastest and longest high-level sorties flown by the RAF in jet aircraft up to that time. The three captains assigned to the Special Duties Flight included Sqn Ldr John Crampton, the second Canberra CO of No 101 Sqn.

The principal aim of the sorties flown by RB-45Cs (at 32,000-42,000 ft) was to obtain radar photographs of potential V-force targets in western Russia. One route ran through Germany to cover targets in the Baltic states, a second route was to the south towards Moscow and the third further south again so as to take in Ukrainian industrial complexes. The flights were deemed to have been successful, although weather and engine troubles delayed the jets' return to Sculthorpe. Later flights were less productive, and on 16 December 1952 C-in-C Bomber Command wrote to the Commander, 7th Air Division, to say 'I am only sorry that the operation ended as it did – without the answers'.

For many years there has been a story that the RAF flew a Canberra B 2 complete with a large, oblique camera deep into Soviet territory in 1953-54 to photograph the Kapustin Yar ballistic missile test site, after which the jet landed in Iran. There is circumstantial evidence that the RAF did indeed fly Canberras over Warsaw Pact territory around this time, and in November 1952 permission was sought from the Norwegian government to operate out of Bodø air base over northwest Russia using 'the new two-engine British jets'. PR 3 squadron ORBs make no mention of any such missions, but these record books were only cleared to Secret so that is not conclusive. Chris Pocock, the foremost authority on U-2 operations and associated spy flights, has documentary evidence that Kapustin Yar was not photographed from the air until September 1957 and, anyway, the idea that the RAF and the USAF collaborated to squeeze a 100-in focal length camera into the aft fuselage of a standard RAF Canberra B 2 is fanciful in the extreme. Why not use a PR 3 for starters?

On 26 March 1953, No 540(PR) Sqn with its black PR 3s moved from Benson to Wyton, near Huntingdon, together with No 58(PR) Sqn with Mosquito PR 35s and No 82(PR) Sqn with Lancaster PR 1s, which started converting to the Canberra PR 3 the following December. These three PR units comprised the UK Photographic Reconnaissance Unit (PRU), which formed part of Bomber Command.

Ken Edmonds was stuck in a pre-OCU supernumerary job at Wyton in 1952 after completing navigation school. He was then detached to No 40 Sqn to act as a safety observer until sent to do a navigation

Navigator Tony Burt (left) and pilot Phil Taylor, who were crewed together flying Canberra PR 7s with No 31 Sqn from Laarbruch in the late 1950s (*Tony Burt*)

refresher course on Varsities at Swinderby. Ken finished top of his class and was duly offered his pick of postings. He chose PR Canberras and was sent to Bassingbourn, and after two weeks he was moved forward two courses to join a pilot whose navigator had been chopped. This pilot was Vic McNabney, who had already done a tour on PR Meteors and, in Ken's words, 'he was an absolute ace'. They joined No 82 Sqn and he and Vic were the first PR crew to make 'Select' at Wyton.

The first unit to equip fully with the Canberra PR 7 was No 542 Sqn, which re-formed at Wyton on 15 May 1954. No 82 Sqn initially operated PR 3s from November 1953, as did No 58 Sqn a month later. No 540 Sqn undertook the PR 7 Intensive Flying Trials, known as 'Seven Up', in June 1954, with No 82 Sqn next to get the PR 7 from October 1954.

'We flew a crew of two on PR, and it was a dream job for a 20-year-old', said Ken Edmonds. 'We did a lot of high altitude photography with our horizon-to-horizon fan of six F52 36-in cameras, and used an F49 for survey work. We flew Ordnance Survey [OS] lines at 16,666 ft or 8333 ft to give the appropriate scale for the OS people, but a lot of the time we would cruise around the Mediterranean photographing North Africa.

'With no upper airways, I would put my straight edge on the map and fly direct from Wyton to Luqa and then perhaps east as far as Habbaniyah, near Baghdad. To reach Habbaniyah from the Canal Zone, we flew to Aqaba, in Jordan, until we saw the pipeline, turned right and flew until we saw a patch of green, which was the irrigation around Habbaniyah. We did no target study and we had no specific war role. We trained in case something came along – I don't remember training for anything in particular.

'We would photograph visually from the nose. As I remember, none of the PR 3s or 7s were fitted with the T2 bombsight. The fore-and-aft "yellow banana" sight was common to all the PR Canberras at Wyton, and the New Zealand Air Race PR 3 in the RAF Museum is still fitted with a "banana" sight. If you hold one finger up about nine inches in front of your eyes, you see double – the nav simply directed the pilot to follow the desired track between the two images! It could not have been less sophisticated, but it worked. One day, we were briefed to fly at 40,000 ft west up the Thames Estuary to beyond Heathrow on behalf of British Rail or the Greater London Council. It was such a gin clear day that I could see my house in south London. We took an incredible set of prints, and I'm sure that one of them was used as the opening shot of *Eastenders* before the Dome was built.'

Across in Germany, Laarbruch, near the Dutch border, housed No 34 Reconnaissance Wing, which was principally composed of three Canberra PR squadrons. No 69(PR) Sqn re-formed in October 1953 with Canberra PR 3s before moving to Laarbruch on 13 December 1954. It was subsequently joined by No 31(PR) Sqn, which re-formed on 1 March 1955 with PR 7s, and the wing was completed by the re-formation of No 80(PR) Sqn with PR 7s the following August. Each Canberra squadron had a Mobile Field Processing Unit attached to it. On 1 June 1956, No 17(PR) Sqn re-formed with PR 7s at Wahn, moving to Wildenrath on 3 April 1957.

The 'high-level' PR Canberras were complimented by the 'low-level' tactical reconnaissance Swifts and Meteor FR 9s based at Gutersloh. However, this was a largely artificial divide. High-level PR was frequently impracticable over the cloudy skies of Europe, and in the words of an *Aeroplane* magazine evaluation of the 2nd Allied Tactical Air Force (ATAF) on 8 June 1956, 'when it is necessary to assess the area of damage caused by atomic weapons against enemy targets, low-level coverage or even visual reconnaissance may be resorted to by PR aircraft in bad visibility'.

Tony Burt did his first navigator tour on Sunderlands, before being posted to PR Canberras in November 1955. At around this time the No 231 OCU PR element of 11 Canberras and 11 Meteors was detached to Merryfield, in Somerset, to spread the workload. Tony recalled;

'My first flight at Merryfield was in PR 3 WE143 with Flt Lt [later ACM] John Gingell on 13 March 1956. I was crewed up with my pilot Phil Taylor, although I didn't fly with Phil until a T 4 refresher exercise on 7 May. Why the refresher? Our PR course should have run for 12 weeks to parallel "the long bomber course", with a new intake every month. However, the tailplane actuator runaway snag that bedevilled the Canberra for a long time had an adverse effect on my OCU course. We had a lot of "gardening leave", which generally took the form of us disappearing off to visit such exotic locations as Lyme Regis, Seaton and Beer.

'We flew our first PR 3 conversion sortie with Flt Lt Hardless (on the Rumbold seat) on 24 July in WE171. On 14 August we progressed from pinpoints to feature line overlaps in PR 3 WE172. Our first "Opex" (navigation and photography), and longest trip of the course, was on 28 August in PR 3 WE150 – 4.40 hours. We progressed to small area cover photography in PR 3 WF923 on 29 August – we were into our

Two brand new Canberra PR 7s of No 31 Sqn are seen in formation during a flight from Laarbruch shortly after joining the unit in 1955. 'Formation flying was a rare event on the squadron,' said Tony Burt, 'and I have only four log book entries referring to such sorties' (*Tony Burt*)

stride by then! Our Final Handling Test was with Flt Lt Hardless on 30 August, then we went on leave pending our departure for Germany.'

Tony and Phil were posted to No 31 Sqn, where 'we converted to PR 7s at Laarbruch – we had the "banana sight", but I found it got in the way. I tended to eyeball everything – I was never a "black box" man.'

No 34 Wing normally engaged in high-level PR sorties from Norway to the Mediterranean. During Exercises *Stronghold* and *Rejuvenate*, Laarbruch Canberras simulated bombing runs during high-level photographic runs on targets such as Birmingham. Now that well-flown Hawker Hunters were in Fighter Command service, the Canberras seemed to be much more vulnerable, although there was an element of 'smoke and mirrors' involved in their interception. 'Boz' Robinson was a young fighter pilot on No 74 Sqn at Horsham St Faith at the time, and in his opinion, 'it was never a problem to intercept a Canberra by Hunter during the annual air defence exercises – I suspect because they were told not to get too high for us!'

Nonetheless, No 34 Wing PR crews felt they would be safer flying right down close to the deck, where ground cover would confer greater protection than performance. Moreover, in Tony Burt's words, 'it was no use photographing from 40,000 ft if the target was under a 2000-ft cloud base. I remember that Exercise *Royal Flush* in 1958 had two parts – low level and a high level – with Canberras doing the high level element. In reality, we were entirely focused on low-level PR training on behalf of 2nd TAF and 4th TAF. We kept well away from the Inner German Border, and if the radar controller advised you that you were getting close, you turned straight away onto a heading of 270 degrees'.

By 1956 some Laarbruch pilots had developed a technique of banking their Canberras to take oblique shots at comparatively low levels.

Exercise *Amled* was a regular fixture to test the Danish air defences, while Exercise *Guest* was generated on a monthly bases in order to test the local air defences in West Germany. The PR Canberras were part of No 83 Group, and they formed the attacking force, tasked with visual and photographic coverage of pre-planned targets. Tony Burt flew two brief *Guest* sorties on 13 December 1956 with Flg Off Peter Thomas. 'First take-off was at 0940 hrs in WJ816, with our target being "former marshalling yards south of Verden" – southeast of Bremen – then a second

Canberra PR 7 WT519 of No 31 Sqn at Gutersloh in 1960. The unit's 'Goldstar' badge was based on the Star of India, as No 31 Sqn claimed to be the first military unit to fly in India – a feat it achieved in late December 1915. WT519 remained in RAF service until the early 1990s (*Peter Green Collection*)

take-off at 1355 hrs in WT511 for target "Hanover airfield". Then on 17 January 1957 I was airborne in WT510 with Flt Lt Ferguson at 1005 hrs to photograph "Minden rail yards"'.

In December 1956, Tony Burt's logbook gave an idea 'of how far we fanned out over northern Europe in our PR training sorties. On the 5th, 14th and 31st I was airborne with different pilots on low-level UK cross-countries. On 6 and 17 December I was airborne on high-level cross-countries over France. And on the 15th and the 17th I was airborne for low-level cross-countries over the British Zone of Germany. 17 December must have been very busy for me, as the French trip was 3 hr 25 min in duration and the second sortie was airborne just under two hours after we landed back! Why so frenetic I have no idea?!'

The PR 3 and PR 7 had the same daylight camera fit. For night work, they carried two F89 cameras plus either a 150 capacity crate of 1.75-in flares or a flare carrier of five 8-in magnesium flares. In the low-level night role, the PR 7 carried two F97 cameras with 5-in lenses designed for night photography at altitudes between 400-2000 ft. Illumination for the exposures was provided by the 1.75-in photoflash cartridges, which were ejected automatically from a discharger at regular intervals, giving an effective exposure time of 1/50th of a second. Both cameras were used to photograph the same strip of ground, with the flashes timed to explode at regular intervals such that the first exposure of one camera overlapped the first exposure of the other camera by 50 per cent, and so on throughout the whole photographic run. The resultant image format was 5-in x 4.5-in, and each camera magazine held 100 ft of film, giving 480 exposures.

All Canberra PR 3 squadrons updated to PR 7s during 1954/55, although there was an element of musical chairs as No 540(PR) Sqn disbanded on 31 March 1956. No 82(PR) Sqn operated PR 7s for barely two years before disbanding on 1 September 1956. That same year, No 13 Sqn became the first Canberra unit in the Mediterranean area, having previously operated Meteor PR 10s at Abu Sueir in the Suez Canal Zone. When the British agreed to evacuate the Canal Zone, No 13 Sqn moved to Akrotiri, in Cyprus, where it received its first two Canberras in May 1956.

While No 13 Sqn was adapting to its new PR Canberras, President Gamal Abdel Nasser started making waves in Egypt. Having accepted weaponry from the USSR, including MiG fighters and Il-28 bombers, he now went in search of finance and specialist help to construct an enormous dam on the upper Nile. Failing to get western support for his Aswan project, Nasser announced on 26 July 1956 that he would nationalise the Suez Canal and use the dues that came from passing world trade to finance the building of his dam.

George Worrall was on No 18 Sqn in July 1956 when 'we were designated for Operation *Alacrity* [a wing of 24 aircraft available to reinforce the RAF's Middle East Air Force (MEAF) in an emergency] and to be trained for shallow dive-bombing in readiness for short-notice deployment overseas. The technique called on the nav/bomb-aimer from his prone position to guide the pilot as he winged over to turn into the target. Once lined up and in a shallow dive, the pilot could then release the bomb load himself. Although we did not know it at the time, we were being earmarked and prepared for the Suez campaign'.

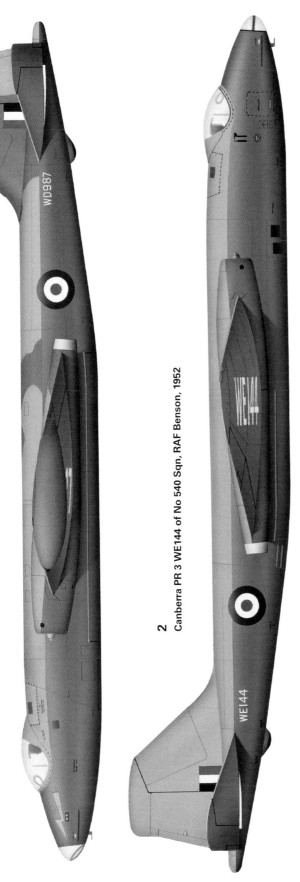

1
Canberra B 2 WD987 of No 12 Sqn, RAF Binbrook, 1952

2
Canberra PR 3 WE144 of No 540 Sqn, RAF Benson, 1952

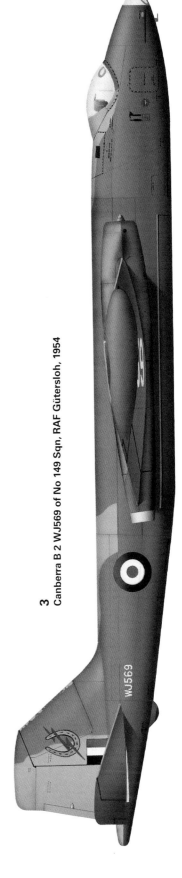

3
Canberra B 2 WJ569 of No 149 Sqn, RAF Gütersloh, 1954

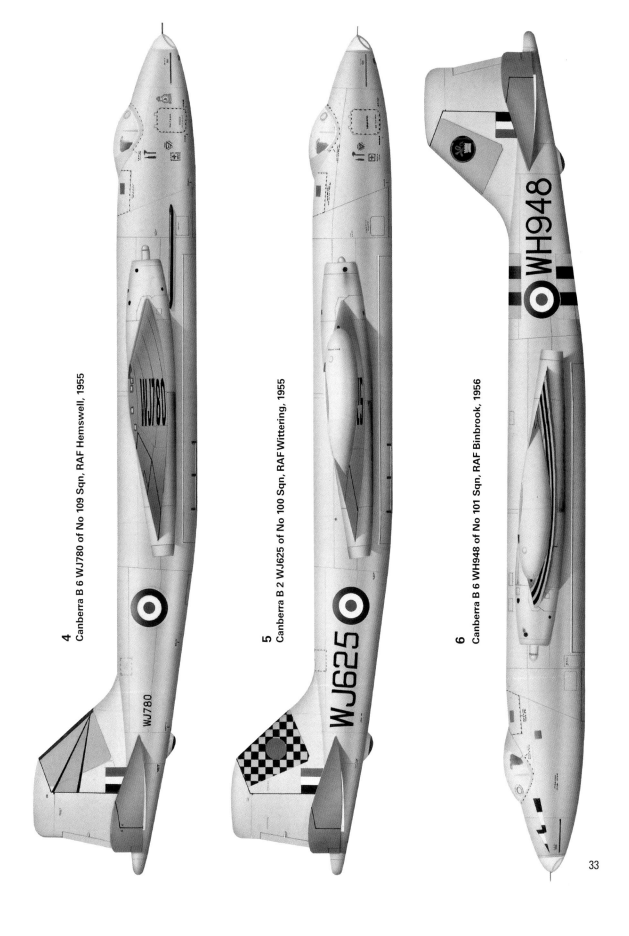

4
Canberra B 6 WJ780 of No 109 Sqn, RAF Hemswell, 1955

5
Canberra B 2 WJ625 of No 100 Sqn, RAF Wittering, 1955

6
Canberra B 6 WH948 of No 101 Sqn, RAF Binbrook, 1956

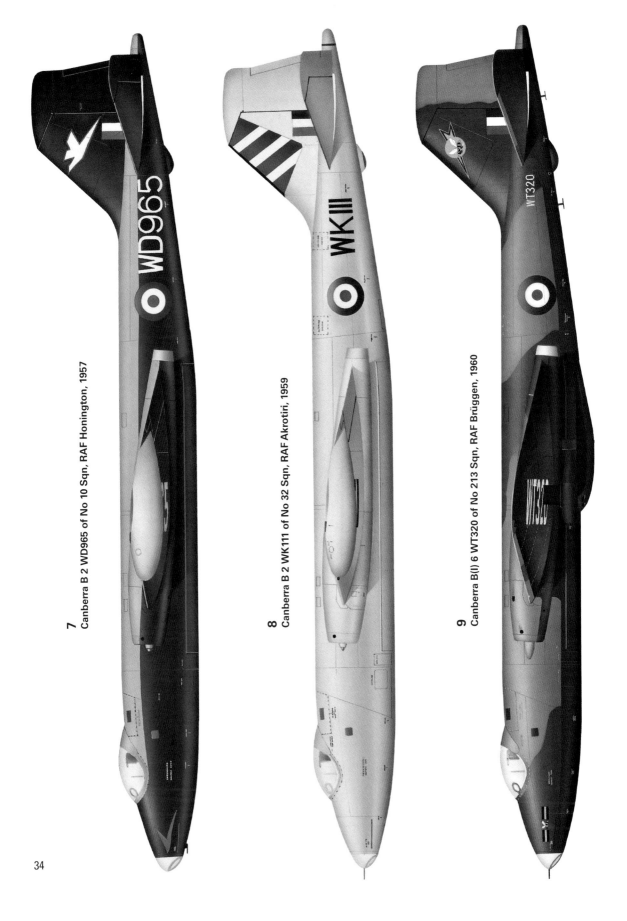

7
Canberra B 2 WD965 of No 10 Sqn, RAF Honington, 1957

8
Canberra B 2 WK111 of No 32 Sqn, RAF Akrotiri, 1959

9
Canberra B(I) 6 WT320 of No 213 Sqn, RAF Brüggen, 1960

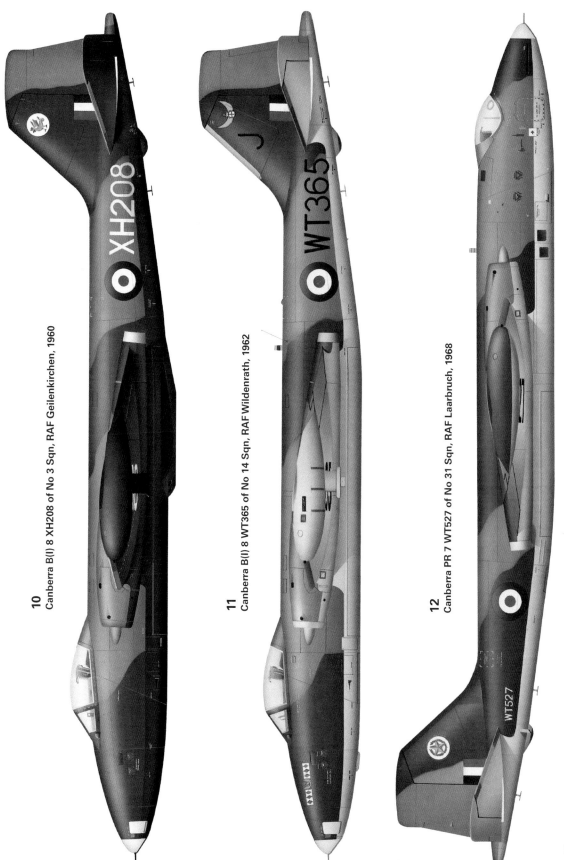

10
Canberra B(I) 8 XH208 of No 3 Sqn, RAF Geilenkirchen, 1960

11
Canberra B(I) 8 WT365 of No 14 Sqn, RAF Wildenrath, 1962

12
Canberra PR 7 WT527 of No 31 Sqn, RAF Laarbruch, 1968

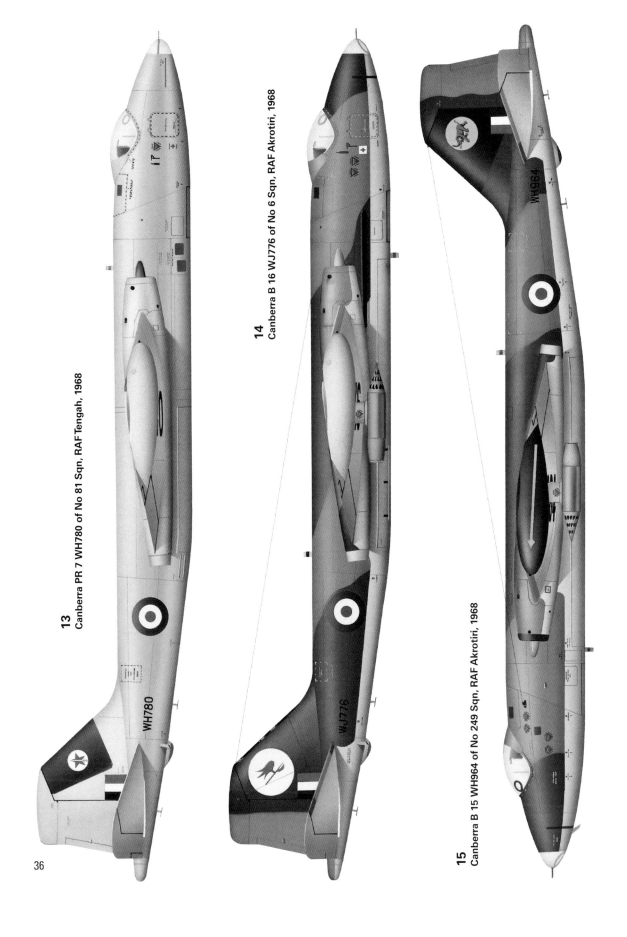

13
Canberra PR 7 WH780 of No 81 Sqn, RAF Tengah, 1968

14
Canberra B 16 WJ776 of No 6 Sqn, RAF Akrotiri, 1968

15
Canberra B 15 WH964 of No 249 Sqn, RAF Akrotiri, 1968

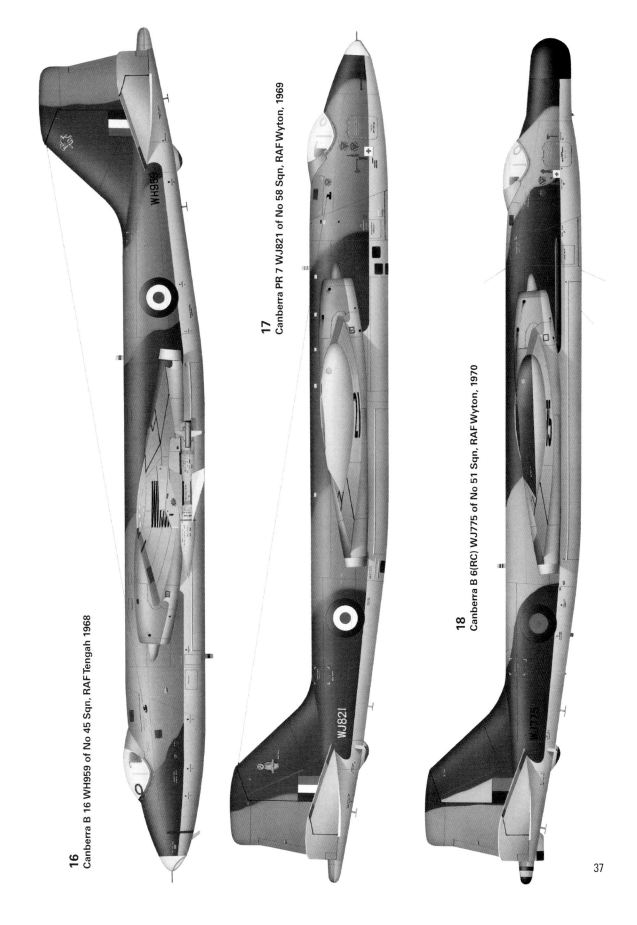

16
Canberra B 16 WH959 of No 45 Sqn, RAF Tengah 1968

17
Canberra PR 7 WJ821 of No 58 Sqn, RAF Wyton, 1969

18
Canberra B 6(RC) WJ775 of No 51 Sqn, RAF Wyton, 1970

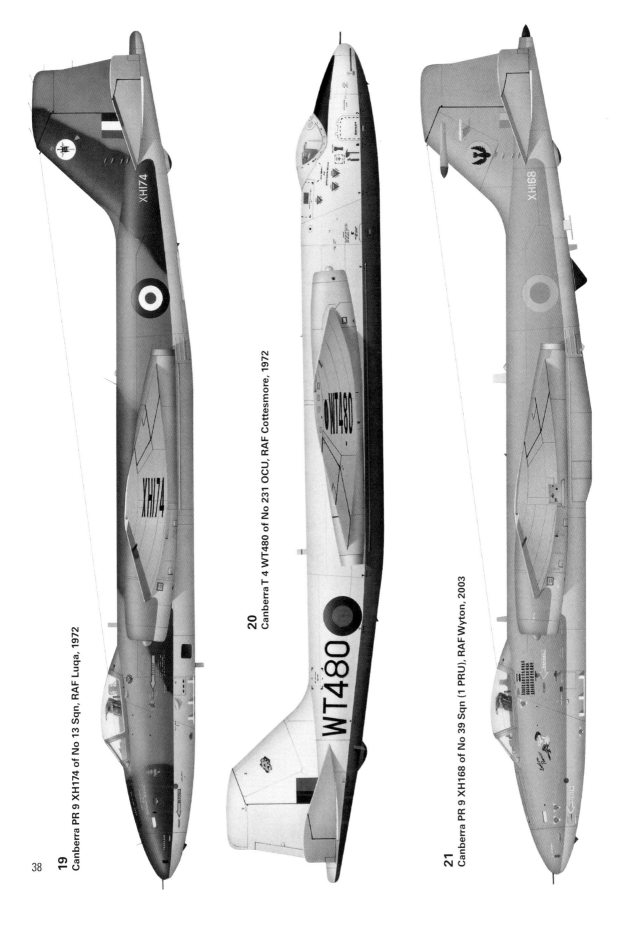

19
Canberra PR 9 XH174 of No 13 Sqn, RAF Luqa, 1972

20
Canberra T 4 WT480 of No 231 OCU, RAF Cottesmore, 1972

21
Canberra PR 9 XH168 of No 39 Sqn (1 PRU), RAF Wyton, 2003

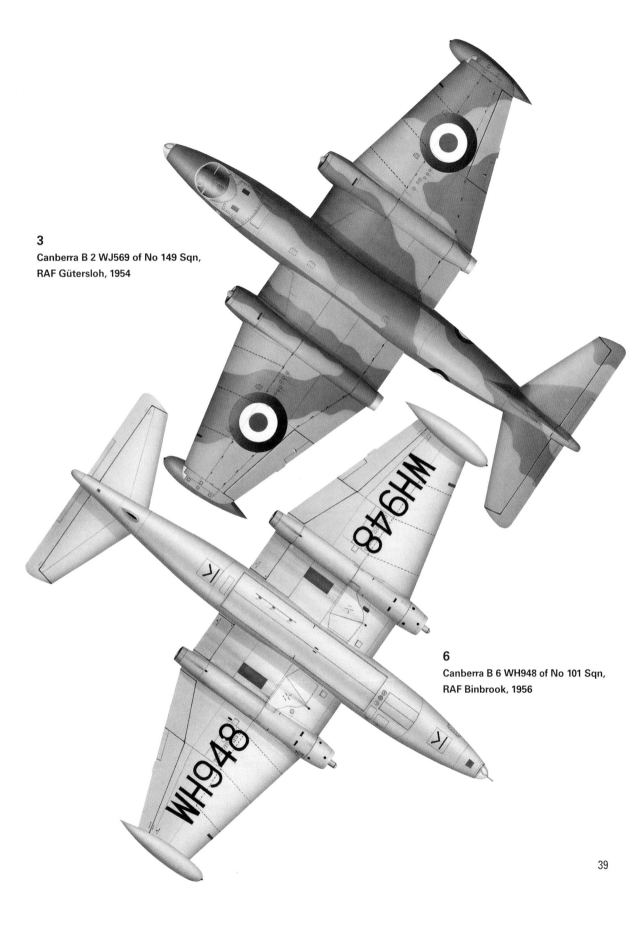

3
Canberra B 2 WJ569 of No 149 Sqn,
RAF Gütersloh, 1954

6
Canberra B 6 WH948 of No 101 Sqn,
RAF Binbrook, 1956

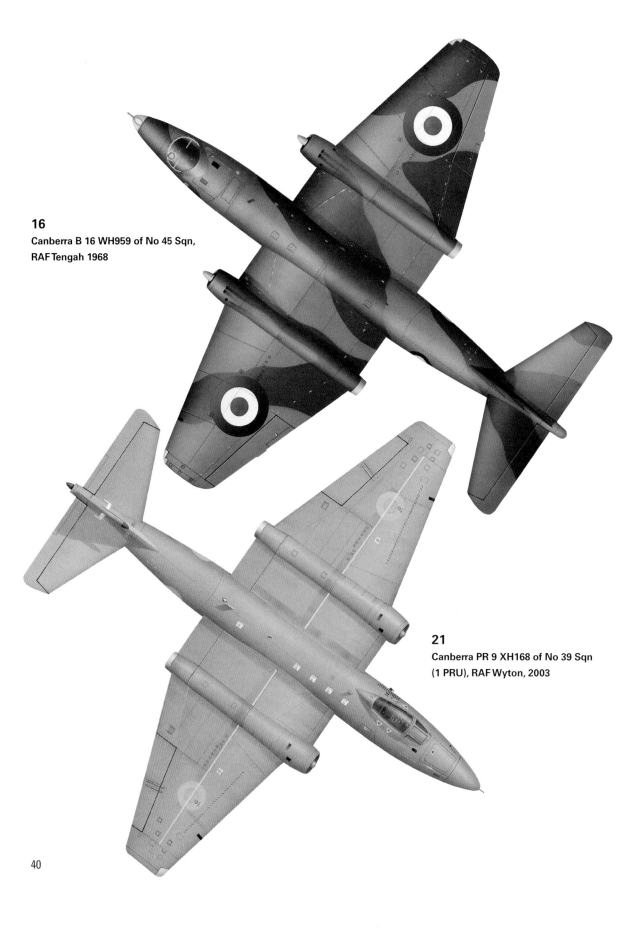

16
Canberra B 16 WH959 of No 45 Sqn,
RAF Tengah 1968

21
Canberra PR 9 XH168 of No 39 Sqn
(1 PRU), RAF Wyton, 2003

THE SUEZ CAMPAIGN

Prime Minister Anthony Eden was scarred by his recollections of appeasement in the 1930s, and he likened Egyptian plans to nationalise the Suez Canal to the occupation of the Rhineland by Germany. Eden was, however, a sick man on a variety of medications who reacted with a frenzy that precluded clarity as to the long-term implications of his actions. When CAS Sir Dermot Boyle returned to the Air Ministry following Nasser's nationalisation of the Suez Canal Company, he opened his address to the air staff with, 'The Prime Minister has gone bananas. He wants us to invade Egypt!'

Working covertly, the British, French and Israelis conspired together. The Anglo-French element was codenamed Operation *Musketeer*: Phase 1 was to neutralise the Egyptian Air Force (EAF); Phase 2 involved air attacks against key points, designed to reduce the Egyptian will to attack; Phase 3 was a joint airborne attack on Port Said and Port Faud to secure a coastal airfield, followed by Phase 4 – a seaborne landing by Royal Marines and French commandos leading to a break out down the Canal to Suez itself.

EAF frontline strength was estimated at 150 jet fighters and 24 jet bombers, divided among three MiG-15, three Vampire, one Meteor and two Il-28 bomber units. A new batch of MiG-17s arrived in early October, with a flight of six aircraft based initially at Almaza. As the EAF did not possess any nightfighters, British attack aircraft were to go in at night until air supremacy was secured.

Phase 1 was to start on 31 October 1956, but knowledge comes before power, and from 1 August No 13 Sqn at Akrotiri was augmented by a No 58 Sqn detachment from Wyton. No 13 Sqn had only four Canberras by September, and the unit's conversion from Meteor PR 10s was affected by technical and maintenance problems, as well as damage inflicted on one of its PR 7s in a landing accident. By September the No 58 Sqn detachment, commanded by Flt Lt Bernie Hunter, consisted of four Canberra PR 7s (WH775, WH779, WH801 and WT540) in anticipation of the covert Suez operation.

MEAF was assured by the UK Chiefs of Staff Committee that the PR squadrons' 'chances of detection are very small. Indeed, apart from some misfortune due to engine failure or a fortuitous interception, the risk of interception can be discounted'. Nonetheless, it made sense to be prepared, and preliminary aerial reconnaissance started on 20 October when a No 58 Sqn Canberra PR 7 flew along the Egyptian coast at a height of 30,000 ft. The mission, which had been specially authorised by the Air Ministry, provoked no apparent Egyptian reaction. Anthony Eden later wrote in his memoirs;

'For some time we had been keeping occasional and informal watch on the Canal and Egyptian troop movements. We had done this by means of Canberras flying high and often a little way out to sea. There had never been any attempted interference with these flights, and we believed them to be unperceived.'

In reality, the EAF was fully aware of them, but had clear instructions from President Nasser not to interfere or provoke the British. No 13/58 Sqn's Canberras were not yet permitted to fly over the Egyptian mainland, but Anglo-French Intelligence Staffs were given high-altitude pictures of the Canal Zone taken from USAF Lockheed U-2s operating out of Turkey.

On 28 October – the day before the Israelis invaded Egypt – the first No 13/58 Sqn sortie to photograph the Suez Canal Zone was captained

Getting ready for Suez, Canberra B 6 WH960 of No 12 Sqn is bombed up at Hal Far, Malta, in October 1956. The standard Canberra internal 6000-lb warload comprised two 'triplets' of 1000-lb bombs. The fox marking on the fin of this aircraft was red in colour (*Peter Green Collection*)

by Flt Lt G J Clark in WJ821. By 1100 hrs in Cairo, according to a confidant of the Egyptian president, 'reports had begun to come in describing how Canberra aircraft were carrying out reconnaissance missions over Lake al-Bardawil, in Sinai, the Suez Canal and Port Said'. The PR 7 was photographing EAF airfields and military movements. The MEAF's sole Canberra PR squadron lacked its own film processing and interpretation equipment, which meant that films had to be sent to Episkopi to be processed and then brought back to Akrotiri, adding three to four hours to the analysis timescale.

The following day at 1150 hrs, still before Israeli paratroopers began dropping near the Mitla Pass in Sinai, Canberra PR 7 WT540, flown by Flt Lt John Field and Flg Off D J Lever, left Akrotiri. It landed back safely at 1600 hrs, despite being fired upon by 'ineffectual AAA'.

In Prime Minster Eden's words, 'late on the evening of the 29th I had a talk with the Minister of Defence and the Chief of Air Staff. I told them how important it was for us to have information upon which we could depend for certain as early as possible the next day. A dawn reconnaissance was ordered by four Canberras flying at a great height, 30,000 to 40,000 ft. They would locate and, if possible, photograph the opposing forces. The Canberras carried out their instructions'.

Thus it was on 30 October that four Canberra PR 7s flew along the Suez Canal at 35,000 ft. Two of the jets were intercepted and attacked during these early morning sorties. One crew, consisting of Flg Offs Jim Campbell and R J Toseland (flying WH801), saw cannon shells from a MiG-15 flash past both sides of their cockpit. The Canberra was hit in its port elevator but managed to escape. The second aircraft (WT540), flown by Flt Lt Hunter, with Flg Off Erquhart-Pullen as his navigator, was also intercepted and fired on, but not hit.

The shock was clear in Eden's memoirs;

'Despite their altitude, all four [Canberras] were located and intercepted and some were fired on. All returned safely to base, but one machine was damaged. This interception was a brilliant piece of work by any standard, and when it was reported to me the next day it gave me grim cause for thought. I kept my own council. In the later fighting the Egyptian Air Force was, by contrast, completely ineffective. I do not know the explanation. Maybe the pilots of another nation were flying MiGs that dawn.'

It was decided that the first wave of British bombing raids would be carried out from higher altitude than originally planned.

What, in heaven's name, were WH801 and WT540 doing down at 35,000 ft? In Ken Edmonds' opinion, 'I can think of no reason whatsoever why they would only be flying at 35,000 ft. The beauty of the PR 7 was that, at that time, no fighters could touch us. I remember doing fighter affiliation with the French Air force, when we were overflying France en route to Malta. Flying at 50,000 ft, we would watch the fighters falling out of the sky trying to reach us'.

Some aircrew remember a form of periscope being fitted to No 13/58 Sqn Canberras utilising the cabin roof sextant mounting. This was not to spot the approach of attacking fighters – a typical fighter attack would have come in from below rather than from above. The periscope was used to check if the Canberra was giving its position away by contrailing. PR 7s carried the Orange Putter tail warning radar. This was a pilot-interpreted device – as a fighter came within firing range astern, the little representative circle on the screen grew wings like a London Transport sign and the pilot knew he had to take evasive action.

One of the problems of flying the PR Canberra on operations was that the pilot concentrated on maintaining a steady platform for photography while the navigator focused on getting the line right and taking the photographs. Because of the MiG interceptions, HQ Cyprus decided to fly future operational PR sorties with an extra crew member aboard to keep a look-out. They would have done better to direct PR Canberras to operate at the optimum altitude they were designed for.

CANBERRA B 6

The increased fuel capacity and uprated engines of the solitary pathfinder Canberra B 5 were applied to the basic bomber to create the B 6, giving the new aircraft an additional range of some 800 miles. Since B 5 VX185 had proven most of the innovations, there was no B 6 prototype, and the first production example (WJ754) flew from Samlesbury on 26 January 1954. Thereafter, the B 6 became the main production version. By the end of 1954 there were 24 Main Force Canberra squadrons totalling 214 aircraft – just 19 of the latter were more powerful B 6s.

Canberra B 6s and crews of No 139 Sqn at Hemswell on 3 August 1955, ready to depart on their goodwill tour of the Caribbean. All of these aircraft have been fitted with horizontal Blue Shadow aerials on their forward fuselages. The sideways-looking Blue Shadow radar gave the navigator a print-out of radar returns at right angles to the right of the aircraft up to a distance of some 60 miles, depending on the height. Each aircraft also boasts a No 139 Sqn fin flash in red and white (*Peter Green Collection*)

Five Valiant bomber squadrons participated in *Musketeer* together with 11 Canberra bomber units – Nos 9, 12, 101 and 109 Sqns (all with B 6s) based on Malta, and Nos 10, 15, 18, 27, 44, 61 and 139 Sqns (all with B 2s, apart from No 139, which operated 12 B 6s in the target marker role) from Cyprus. In all, there were 24 Valiants and 91 Canberras assigned to the operation, in addition to the seven PR 7s of No 13/58 Sqn. Bob Hodges, OC Malta Bomber Wing, recalled the uncertainty of it all. 'When we

Canberra B 2s of No 61 Sqn en route from Cyprus to Egypt during the Suez campaign. The pilot of WH907, which sports black and yellow 'Suez stripes', is Flg Off M Freeston. The black semicircle in the foreground is the direct vision (DV) window that allowed the pilot to see outside with some forward vision even if the forward windscreen became opaque from being shattered due to a bird strike or from icing up. The pilot could also take photographs through the DV window (*Peter Green Collection*)

came to be deployed to Malta in October 1956', he said, 'we didn't know until 24 hours before operations commenced whether we were going to bomb the Egyptians or the Israelis'.

With so many aircraft crammed on Cyprus, fear of a Pearl Harbor-style attack led CAS to declare 'the use of Suez airfields by Egyptian aircraft to be totally unacceptable'. Consequently, in Anthony Eden's words, 'The first phase was to consist of the elimination of the Egyptian air force, if possible on the ground, by bombing from Cyprus, Malta and Aden, and by fighter attacks from carriers and from Cyprus. We hoped also in this phase to put Cairo radio out of action and to sink as many Egyptian blockships as possible by pinpoint bombing before they took up blocking positions in the canal'.

A Valiant equipped with the Navigation and Bombing System Mk 1 was to lead each attack and drop a red proximity marker on the selected target. Canberras operating out of Cyprus would then fly in at low level, using the light from the proximity markers to identify the actual target and drop green markers to act as the aiming point for the bomber force. The lead Canberra would direct the main force to drop visually on the green marker. This was not the most accurate way of depositing gravity bombs from around 40,000 ft, but as the targets were well outside the range of any Gee-H station, there was no other option.

The first attack was to be made on Cairo West by Valiants and Canberras from Malta, together with Canberras from Cyprus, to prevent Il-28s from getting airborne. There was a kerfuffle over opening the bomb dumps at Malta on a Saturday, so Hodges ordered the gates to be broken down. Notwithstanding, four Canberra B 6s of No 139 Sqn lifted off from Nicosia at 1715 hrs on 31 October 1956.

The B 6 was cleared to drop 4.5-in parachute flares and 250-lb target indicators. No 139 Sqn's B 6s had a sideways-looking radar called Blue Shadow, which gave the navigator a print-out of radar returns at right angles to the right of the aircraft up to a distance of some 60 miles, depending on the height. In the words of OC No 139 Sqn, Paul Mallorie, 'we had no operational directives on the use of this equipment, but we presumed that all would be revealed when necessary. We used it partly because we had groundcrew who were trained to service it and partly because it was quite fun to operate'.

Seven months earlier, in March 1956, a No 139 Sqn detachment had flown to Libya to devise a low-level target-illumination and marking technique. 'On our own initiative', said Mallorie, 'we tried out low-level Blue Shadow navigation as a means of reaching targets and, as I recall, we had no operational or intelligence staff guidance and were left entirely to our own devices. Our trials were curtailed by Easter, but we did develop a procedure involving two illuminating and two marking aircraft, and that technique was modified in August when mixed loads of flares and target indicators were approved. Four aircraft in the marking team then carried eight flares and two target illuminators each'.

Clive Elton had joined No 139 Sqn at Binbrook on 29 May 1956;

'At that time No 139 Sqn was the only marker unit in Bomber Command. Training involved visual bombing, with the observer in the nose using the standard bombsight, Gee-H bombing controlled by the navigator plotter and shallow dive-bombing, which was very much the pilot's responsibility – and delight! We used a number of different bombing ranges around the country such as Donna Nook, Jurby, Wainfleet and Chesil Bank.

'My crew became operational just in time for a detachment to Luqa on 22 September 1956. Returning to Binbrook on 18 October, I was about to set out for home when, at 1900 hrs, we were recalled to the squadron to be informed that as an *Alacrity* squadron, we were to depart the next morning for Nicosia. Although very junior (or perhaps for that very reason), I was to be first away at 0700 hrs on the 19 October.'

At Nicosia, No 139 Sqn was brought up to full strength with 12 B 6s and 14 three-man crews.

Paul Mallorie recalled that 'on 29 or 30 October, we received our first intelligence briefing. I would like to emphasise that we had had no target briefing or given any consideration to target defences when we were developing the marking technique that was about to be put to the test. Intelligence material at our level was surprisingly sparse – we had very dim, rather foggy, pictures of airfields. The initial operations were planned, and then delayed for a day'. WT371, captained by Flt Lt John Slater, was to be the lead aircraft, but as he was about to taxi out from the dispersal there was a hammering on the entry hatch of his aircraft. It was opened and the crew informed that they were to attack Almaza airfield rather than Cairo West.

Out over the Mediterranean, six No 138 Sqn Valiants were en route to crater runways at Cairo West airfield just as Vulcan 'Black Buck 1' did at Port Stanley in 1982. Up at 42,000 ft, the Valiant crews were blithely unaware that Prime Minister Eden was being told by the US Ambassador that American citizens were being evacuated along the desert road that passed very close to Cairo West. Meanwhile, the transmitter on the roof of the British Embassy in Cairo was passing word back to London that 15 US transport aircraft were

Canberra B 2s of No 27 Sqn rub shoulders with Valettas of No 114 Sqn at Nicosia during the Suez conflict (*Peter Green Collection*)

waiting at Cairo West to evacuate American nationals. Panic gripped Whitehall and frantic W/T messages were dispatched via the Cyprus forward relay station to delete Cairo West from the list of targets.

In Bob Hodges' words, 'as the first wave of Valiants was on its way to Cairo, this created enormous problems because there were four or five subsequent waves due to take off immediately afterwards. I initiated an immediate recall of the first wave on W/T but, in addition, the routeing of the aircraft was very near to El Adem, and they were able to give a verbal instruction by R/T in plain language to recall these aircraft'. Hodges then faced a situation where the first wave of Valiants was returning to Luqa with full bomb loads and further waves were taking off. 'We had to have the bombs jettisoned, and you can imagine the problems of landing these aircraft, with others taking off, on a single runway'. The seven Canberras of Nos 12 and 109 Sqns that had taken off with the Valiants from Malta had also been given the new target of Almaza airfield, but they were then held back.

Further east in Cyprus, it was fortunate that John Slater's navigator had Almaza marked on his map. The marker force was scheduled to take off after the main force had departed, hence the motto 'I must hurry and catch up with them, for I am their leader'. As John Slater said to waiting journalists afterwards, 'we were in fact 30 seconds late after a 25-minute flight. With other Canberras we flew high over the target. There was no fighter resistance, but there was some light flak up to 8000 ft. The airfield we attacked was beautifully lit up. There were many aeroplanes on it'.

Seven immaculate Canberra B 6s from No 12 Sqn sit at Hal Far on the eve of the Suez crisis. WH951 lacks a unit emblem on its fin, this aircraft having been hastily supplied to No 12 Sqn by No 9 Sqn just prior to the Malta deployment. The bomber was destined not to return to Binbrook after the conflict had ended, for on 7 March 1957 WH951's brakes failed on landing at Luqa and it overshot the runway and hit a wall (*Peter Green Collection*)

More Canberra B 6s at Hal Far in October 1956. The five aircraft in the front row closest to the camera are from No 101 Sqn, with the remaining four jets being No 9 Sqn B 6s. The Canberras in the second row are all from No 12 Sqn (*Peter Green Collection*)

Slater's crew were known as 'Marker 1', and with his bomb-aimer, Flg Off Geoffrey Harrop, they were expected to drop their eight 4.5-in flares from 8000 ft, then break to port and orbit at 4000 ft. 'Marker 2', Flt Lt N M North's crew in WT369, followed suit before orbiting at 5000 ft. Two follow-on No 139 Sqn aircraft carried just 12 flares each. Once the target was illuminated and identified, the marker crews went into a shallow dive to place their Target Indicators (TIs) – Slater and North's aircraft carried two TIs each.

In the words of Flt Sgt Mike Heather, the 'Marker 2' navigator in WT369, 'the Egyptian gunners seemed to shoot at the flares rather than us, so marking the target was easy, although by the time we had finished all the lights had been turned out'. The other two marker aircraft, WJ768 and WJ778, released their flares over the target that had been identified, whereupon seven Canberras from Nos 10, 15, 44 and 139 Sqns dropped 41 1000-lb bombs. On landing back at Nicosia, the crews reported that the marker was on the aiming point, and that their bombs had straddled hangars, runway and hardstandings. Unfortunately, they were on the wrong airfield, the force bombing Cairo International by mistake.

Although the proximity of Almaza to Cairo International was a contributory factor, in the words of Air Cdre David Lee, who was then Secretary to the Chiefs of Staff Committee, 'the mistake would never have been made by experienced crews had the normal time for flight planning been available to them'. It was an inauspicious beginning.

Five Valiants of No 148 Sqn and one from No 214 Sqn departed Luqa in the late afternoon of 31 October to arrive over Almaza at 2000 hrs, together with four Canberra B 6s of No 109 Sqn and three B 6s of No 12 Sqn from Luqa/Hal Far. Visual marking was undertaken by four No 139 Sqn Canberras, which were tasked to fly over the target at low level and drop red TIs – the bombers at 30,000 ft were then to release into these. The aiming points were the runway intersections, and a total of 104 1000-lb bombs were dropped. Crews were briefed to avoid the camp areas, and instructions were given that bombs were not to be jettisoned 'live' to avoid Egyptian casualties. In the event, post-attack PR showed that some fell short and one even exploded in the centre of the parade ground

of the barracks nearby. One of the Canberras was held by a searchlight over the target area but the crew was able to evade successfully.

It was an 1800-mile round trip from Malta, which explained why the shorter-range B 2s were based in Cyprus. Even so, No 109 Sqn B 6 WJ781, flown by Flt Lt I N Wilson, suffered a faulty fuel line from a tip tank and was flying on fumes by the time it squeaked into Hal Far.

Kabrit airfield was the target for the third attack on 31 October/ 1 November when seven Canberra B 2s from Cyprus (Nos 10, 15 and 44 Sqns), plus four marker aircraft from No 18 Sqn, were joined by seven No 101 Sqn B 6s from Malta. The departure of the bombers from Nicosia at 2300 hrs was witnessed by journalist George Evans;

'I stood on the airfield and watched the bomber force take off at regular intervals of a few minutes. One after another the Canberras roared down the runway, their twin engines emitting an ear-piercing whistle, climbed high into the night sky and set course for the Egyptian coast, which is only about half-an-hour's flying time from Cyprus. Overhead, silhouetted against a rich canopy of stars, other Canberras, their [Alamaza] mission completed, circled the airfield and touched down.'

A total of 32 1000-lb bombs were dropped on Kabrit, all of which were assessed as falling within 450 yards of the marker. At least three MiGs on the ground were claimed as destroyed.

Next on the target list was the airfield at Abu Sueir. The Nav Radar in the lead No 138 Sqn Valiant at 42,000 ft identified the target and, after a steady run, declared, 'Target Indicator away'. The sky was illuminated by the red proximity marker, and shortly afterwards the Canberra pilot came on the radio, 'Identified the target'. The sky was lit up again, but this time by the green marker, followed by instructions from the Canberra pilot, 'Bomber Force bomb on the green marker'. The Malta force was joined in the attack on Abu Sueir by five Canberra B 2s from Cyprus belonging to Nos 10, 15, 44 and 61 Sqns. Markers were dropped from four B 2s from No 18 Sqn. No enemy opposition, either by fighters or anti-aircraft fire, was encountered.

The fifth, and final, raid of the night launched from Nicosia at 0500 hrs. The target was Inchas,

Posing for the No 61 Sqn Christmas card at Upwood on 9 October 1957, each of these Canberra B 2s bears a red Lincoln imp emblem on the tail. No 61 Sqn disbanded on 31 March 1958 (*Peter Green Collection*)

Canberra PR 7 WH801 of No 13 Sqn, crewed by Flg Offs Jim Campbell and R J Toseland, was targeted by an Egyptian MiG-15 over Inchas during a post-raid night photo-reconnaissance mission on 1 November 1956. The crew was quite disturbed to see explosive shells fired from a fighter 'sail by the cockpit on both sides from the rear'. The aircraft is seen here being repaired at Akrotiri (*Peter Green Collection*)

and eight No 27 Sqn Canberras, led by Wg Cdr Peter Helmore, were followed into the darkness by five from No 61 Sqn, plus two No 139 Sqn marker aircraft. There should have been seven Canberras from No 61 Sqn, but two failed to take off, one of which (WH915) suffered an undercarriage retraction on the taxiway. It was impossible to raise the Canberra undercarriage while the mainwheel legs were compressed by the aircraft's weight without deliberately rotating the override collar on the UP button through 90 degrees. It was believed that the pilot was registering his dissent over the Suez operation, and Flg Off Dennis Kenyon was duly court martialled and sentenced to 12 months imprisonment 'for not carrying out a warlike operation with the utmost exertion'. The second Canberra (WH918) got stuck behind WH915 and could not get airborne in time to join the others.

All the bombers returned safely, although one Canberra was intercepted, though not attacked, over the target area by an EAF Meteor NF 13. So much for the Egyptians not operating at night! Subsequent PR revealed that the bombing effort on the first night had not been very effective. Aircraft parked around the airfields seemed intact, and although some runways were cratered, most appeared to be still operational. To add insult to injury, two PR Canberras from No 13 Sqn came under attack. The crew of one, Flg Offs Jim Campbell and R J Toseland in WH801, were quite disturbed to see explosive shells fired from a MiG-15 'sail by the cockpit on both sides from the rear'.

Clive Elton's first two operational sorties were to Luxor, where the Egyptians had moved their aircraft believing that they were out of RAF range;

'A night raid on 1 November was highly successful from the marking point of view. The team consisted of four aircraft, namely "Marker 1" (who was also the bomber leader, in this case Sqn Ldr Terry Kearns), "Marker 2", "Flare 1" and "Flare 2". We were very fortunate in having Terry Kearns, with his masses of World War 2 experience, leading us young guys, and we departed from Nicosia at, I think, two-minute intervals (it may have been one minute), with a similar spacing for time on target.

'"Marker 1" and "2" each had six flares and two 500-lb TIs, but with target marking, you first had to find the target. "Marker 1" would fly in at 8000 ft from a known point – in this case, a bend in the Nile – with flare release after a timed run. The two "Marker" aircraft then dived through the flares to drop their TIs as near as possible to the centre of the airfield. Red and green were the two colours used – I never knew whether the colour chosen had any particular significance.

'As very much the junior boy, I was "Flare 2". "Flare" aircraft just had 12 parachute flares, which we were to drop either on time or, if the target was already illuminated, to back up those already floating down. A 30-40 degree dive was steep enough, with the nav shouting out every 100 ft in the descent. You had to release at 1200 ft, and you dropped when the target appeared just above the cockpit coaming. "Marker 1" had to stick around until he reached his fuel limits, but I just headed back to Nicosia.'

Although the marking was accurate, the main force proved ineffective from 30,000 ft, with most of their bombs falling in the desert, so it was decided to repeat the raid in daylight the next day. Clive Elton recalled;

'In daylight you kept the target just to the left of the nose, and at the right moment you dived and rolled from 4000 ft. When dropping a 25-lb practice bomb over a UK range, we were accurate to within 25 yards. For the daylight Luxor raid, the "Marker" aircraft carried a mixed load of TIs and 1000-lb bombs. We (nominally the two flare aircraft) had six 1000-lb bombs that we dropped from 10,000 ft using the visual bombing technique. The main force bombed from high level again.

'We knew our target in the morning because the BBC announced which places Egyptians should stay away from! On 3 November I teamed up with John Slater, and we two flew at low level over sea and sand, by day, to mark and bomb Almaza Camp. We each had two 500-lb TIs and three 1000-lb bombs. This mission included some dive-bombing, during which the Egyptians had the impertinence to shoot at us with what I presume was light ack-ack. It did produce puffs of black smoke nearby, but not too near.'

Paul Mallorie recalled the second attack on Luxor airfield;

'On that occasion, the marker aircraft [WT370] carried a mixed load of TIs and 1000-lb bombs, which were proximity fused. I'm sure Boscombe knew nothing about that. Having dive-bombed with TIs at last light, we were supposed to then see the raid through and add our contribution of straight and level attacks with 1000 pounders. By that time, the gyros had completely toppled, the navigators were confused and the bombsights useless. So we made dive-bomb attacks on the parked Il-28 "Beagles" that were there, with high explosives.'

After it was announced at 0800 hrs on 2 November that Phase 1 – neutralisation of the EAF – had been achieved, the way was clear to mount an air offensive by day. The last No 139 Sqn operation marked the Suez dropping zone near Port Said on 5 November. 'That was it for me', said Clive Elton, 'just as we were all getting into the swing of it. However, we stayed on in Nicosia until departing back to Binbrook on 22 December'.

As a precaution against renewed activity, 20 Valiants and 24 Canberras were held at various states of readiness in the UK.

The official Operation *Musketeer* report covering 31 October to 6 November 1956 listed 24 Valiants flying from Luqa, 29 Canberras based at Luqa and Hal Far and 59 Canberras operating out of Nicosia. During six days of combat, a total of 259 sorties were flown and 1962 bombs – mostly 1000 pounders – dropped. Eighteen raids were made on 13 targets, including Abu Sueir, Almaza, Cairo West, Fayid, Kabrit, Kasfareet and Luxor airfields, together with Cairo Radio Station and the Huckstep barracks, where Egyptian Army tanks and other vehicles were stored, El Agami Island (where a submarine repair depot was believed to be located) and Nifisha marshalling yards. Nicosia's Canberras alone logged 266 operational sorties.

Weather conditions over Egypt were excellent throughout, yet Suez did little to enhance the prestige of the British bomber force. By the time the ceasefire came into effect on the sixth day, three out of the seven main Egyptian airfields were still fully serviceable, another had had its take-off run only partly reduced and a fifth needed only three craters to be filled to be fully serviceable. Ironically, the only airfield completely out of action was Cairo West, and the Egyptians did that to themselves by exploding demolition charges on the runway to prevent Anglo-French landings. Subsequent operational research showed that the total of 942 tons of bombs dropped by the entire Air Task Force during the Suez operation

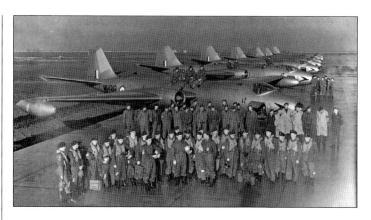

Canberra B 2s, aircrew and groundcrew of No 18 Sqn come together for a group photograph at Upwood in January 1956 (*Peter Green Collection*)

would have been insufficient to neutralise one airfield. Most of the destruction of the EAF was carried out by ground forces.

The *Musketeer* report said bluntly that 'in July 1956 Bomber Command was not constituted for major overseas operations'. The Canberras that formed the bulk of the deployed force were 'equipped only with Gee-H as a blind-bombing device, and there were no Gee-H beacons in the Middle East.

Moreover, it was not possible to position ground-based beacons to give coverage for this equipment over Egypt. Lacking Green Satin, the Canberras had to rely entirely on DR [dead reckoning] navigation monitored by visual pinpoints and, in a few cases, by radio compass bearings. This was a handicap to the Malta Canberras operating at ranges near their operational radius of action at night, but navigation of Nicosia-based aircraft on their relatively short sorties was not seriously affected. The Canberras' bombing capability was reduced to visual bombings of target indicators in good weather only. As it was considered prudent for the early attacks to be made at night, this necessitated a reversion to the marking technique successfully used in World War 2.'

The conclusion drawn was that if 'limited war' bomber operations were again to be mounted 'it is considered essential that the Canberra force should have an all-weather bombing and navigation capability that are independent of ground stations'.

When the crisis occurred, Bomber Command was capable of sending two Canberra *Alacrity* squadrons to reinforce the MEAF at 96 hours' notice. The remainder of the Command 'could not undertake such operations' pending the positioning of the necessary equipment and supplies and the preparation of additional marker aircraft and crews to enable the force to operate independently of Gee-H. The report said that no up-to-date photographs and intelligence on targets were available for briefing marker crews and marking equipment was inadequate – no flare clusters were available, which meant that old type flares had to be used. Nevertheless, 'the marker technique was successful, and 50 per cent of all bombs plotted fell within 650 yards of the target'.

JET DOWN

No 13/58 Sqn Canberra PR 7s flew eight sorties on 6 November – the last day of the campaign. There was a regular Syrian PR 'milk run' over Lattakia, Aleppo and Homs to within five kilometres of Damascus, and then a turn westward over Beirut and back towards Cyprus. The PR 7s generally followed the same flightpath to photograph Syrian, Iraqi and Lebanese airfields, and shortly after 0800 hrs, the Syrian frontier post at Abu Kamal, on the River Euphrates, reported a British Canberra was operating at extreme range from Cyprus. Lt Hafiz al-Asad, the future President of Syria, was sent in pursuit, but he was only able to open fire from a distance before the Canberra escaped towards Cyprus.

At the time, the Syrian Air Force had one squadron of Meteor F 8s, mainly based at al-Mezze airfield southwest of Damascus. The PR 7 crew pursued by al-Asad had found their targets covered with cloud, and on their return they reported being 'chased by Meteors in unidentified markings'. Despite having lost the precious element of surprise, Air HQ in Cyprus insisted that a second Canberra immediately be sent to get the required photographs of Syrian airfields and a nearby oil pipeline. Flt Lt Bernie Hunter decided to fly this sortie with Flg Off Roy Erquhart-Pullen as his navigator in WH799. The third member of the crew was Flt Lt Sam Small, another Canberra pilot, who had come out to reinforce the squadron during the Suez crisis, and who provided another pair of eyes up front.

Bernie Hunter recalled that 'we went off [at 1230 hrs] to photograph Riyaq [in the Lebanon], Aleppo [Nairab air base] and al-Rashid [near Baghdad, in Iraq]. Navigation was extremely good, under cloud cover, then towards 12,000 ft, then slowly down to 10,000 ft in order to get overlaps'. The Canberra was reported by telephone entering Syrian airspace over Lattakia, and Syrian Meteors took off as the Canberra passed Aleppo. There was low cloud over Damascus at that time of the morning, and the Syrian fighter pilots were directed to stay hidden in these clouds. Once the Canberra had passed over Homs, they were directed to climb out of the clouds and attack.

As Bernie Hunter recalled, 'we were heading towards Damascus when, to our horror – blue sky! Normally a pilot's dream, but under operating conditions we were, to say the least, in a very unenviable position. My first reaction was to climb on full power to get back into cloud cover, as it would have been absolutely fatal if we had tried to go over Damascus airfield at that height and speed. At about the same time Sam Small warned of a pair of Meteors coming from port or starboard – I can't remember which, but I had to turn towards them. It went on like this for a few minutes, which seemed like several hours, and during the first attack we did not get hit. Then Sam said almost immediately after the first attack, with us still climbing, that another pair were coming in, so we turned again. I turned towards them, and that's when the starboard engine was hit.

'I had been calling Roy, who was in the prone position to take photographs, to come back to the Rumbold seat. He got the message,

No 18 Sqn Canberra B 2s WH919, WJ751, WJ752 and WH920 contrail while in line abreast formation in January 1956. The unit disbanded a year after this photograph was taken in preparation for its re-equipment with Valiant B 1s (*Peter Green Collection*)

I think, but did not come back. Eventually, it got to the stage where I was rapidly losing control of the situation, with one engine out, still burning. I told Sam to get out, and from the rear navigation position he ejected quite safely. I never did contact Roy on the R/T. Since the ejection seat had gone, I assume he tried to bail out. I think I heard a big thud on the aircraft, which could have been Roy's body hitting the tailplane. I then ejected. It seemed only seconds before I hit the ground and broke my left ankle. I didn't know whether I had got out over the Lebanon or not, my mind revolving around the fact that if I was in Syria they were not going to be very friendly.'

In fact, Hunter's Canberra crashed just inside Syrian territory, while he and Sam Small landed just on the Lebanese side of the frontier. The crowd that gathered around him after he landed assumed he was an Israeli and started to rough him up until an English-speaking local teacher told them to leave him alone. Hunter then explained he was from the RAF, whereupon things quietened down. The teacher handed Hunter over to the border post, where he was interrogated by a Syrian officer. He and Sam Small, who was brought in soon after, claimed that they had been doing a weather reconnaissance over Lebanon and had become lost. The two survivors were taken to a hospital in Beirut, from where, after a visit by the British deputy air attaché in Lebanon, both were spirited away in a small boat to Cyprus. As Hunter feared, Roy Erquhart-Pullen was killed when the Canberra crashed.

Looking back, it was inexcusable to send a PR Canberra towards Damascus – air defences tend to concentrate around capital cities – at 10,000 ft in daylight when the element of surprise had been lost. If the task had to be done at all, it should have been given to a tactical reconnaissance jet. This would mark the last time that an RAF crew in an RAF aircraft was shot down in air-to-air combat, and the whole sorry episode typified an overly confident RAF command attitude that had forgotten many of the hard-learned lessons of World War 2.

Hostilities ended at midnight on 6 November 1956, by which time the Canberra PR 7s of No 13/58 Sqn had flown 44 operational missions for the loss of one aircraft. Reconnaissance flights continued over Syria after the conflict had officially ended but, with the loss of WH799, they were escorted by Hunters as they withdrew from the target areas. During 1957/58, one of No 13 Sqn's tasks was to provide photographic coverage of airfields in those Middle Eastern countries that were being supplied with Soviet aircraft, and also to look at new or modernised airfields. Flightpaths were described as 'Routes designated One, Two' and so on in the ORB, and many post-Suez Canberra missions were aborted when contrails were visible up to 50,000 ft.

Stirring though the Suez campaign was when it came to dropping live bombs, it was peripheral to the *raison d'être* of the British bomber arm. In a brooding overview on the lessons of Suez during his last days as Prime Minister, Anthony Eden concluded that the UK needed 'a smaller force that is more mobile and more modern in its equipment'. That aside, his main observation was that 'it is of the first importance to maintain deterrent power, which means the ability to deliver a destructive weapon, atomic or hydrogen, on the target'. And the proving of that British nuclear weaponry was about to begin.

GOING NUCLEAR

The first British operational nuclear weapon was Blue Danube which, like the atomic bombs dropped on Hiroshima and Nagasaki, had a yield of around 10 kilotons (KT). Blue Danubes were slow to roll off the production line, and by the end of 1954 the stock was just five. A Working Party on the Operational Use of Atomic Weapons chaired by the MoD's chief scientist assessed that they would not be powerful enough to destroy the UK's primary targets in the USSR 'such as airfields or ports with a single bomb. The possession of a bomb in the 5-10 megaton [MT] range offers this possibility and would go a long way towards overcoming the need for improved terminal accuracy'. On 16 June 1954, the British government decided 'to initiate a programme for the production of hydrogen bombs'.

A Bomber Command Memorandum issued on 12 May 1956 stated that live nuclear tests overseas would begin with Operation *Mosaic*, involving ground-detonated bursts in the Montebello Islands, off Western Australia. This would be followed by Operation *Buffalo*, an air drop of an atomic weapon at Maralinga, in South Australia, and then Operation *Grapple*, involving air drops over a target in the Pacific Ocean. The principal bomber forces involved in these trials were to be No 76 Sqn Canberra B 6s to support *Mosaic*, *Buffalo* and *Grapple*, No 100 Sqn Canberra PR 7s to support *Grapple* only and No 49 Sqn to supply two Valiant B 1s for *Buffalo* and eight for *Grapple*. By the end of *Grapple* the UK expected to have enough information to produce a freefall H-bomb for the V-force, a megaton warhead for the Blue Steel stand-off missile and a warhead for the Blue Streak ballistic missile.

The first *Mosaic* nuclear tests used a B 2 (WH738) with a modified starboard wingtip tank to trap nuclear particles. What was known as Operation *Hotbox* provided valuable experience about aircrew safety and aircraft contamination, and No 1323 Flt was then established at Wyton with six B 2s as a dedicated nuclear sampling unit. In February 1954 it deployed four B 2s to RAAF Laverton, in Western Australia, to sample tests conducted by the US at Bikini Atoll. During what was known as Operation *Dogstar*, WH738 went missing after its radio compass failed on a transit flight (with another B 2) from Momote to Kwajalein, in the Marshall Islands, on 23 February 1954 with the loss of three crew.

On 1 November 1955 No 1323 Flt was re-designated No 542 Sqn and moved to Weston Zoyland, near Bridgwater, Somerset, to prepare for the next series of *Mosaic* tests in Australia. No 76 Sqn had re-formed at Wittering with Canberra B 2s in December 1953, and it too moved to Weston Zoyland on 15 November 1955 to become a specialist air-sampling unit. No 76 Sqn started

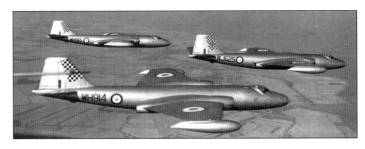

No 100 Sqn Canberra B 2s fly in formation over East Anglia in October 1955. The fin markings comprised the yellow and blue checks of the Wittering Canberra Wing with a green disc for No 100 Sqn in the centre. No 100 Sqn replaced its B 2s with a mixed fleet of B 6s and PR 7s in August 1956 (*Peter Green Collection*)

converting to B 6s in December 1955, and by the following May there was a No 76 Sqn detachment at Edinburgh Field, near Adelaide. On 11 October 1956, Sqn Ldr Ted Flavell's crew in Valiant WZ366 dropped a Blue Danube 'within 110 yards of the aiming point', while No 76 Sqn measured the yield of the atmospheric nuclear detonation.

Delivering a practical Blue Danube was a dress rehearsal for *Grapple* trials to be held in the Pacific a year later. A survey in 1955 selected Captain James Cook's Christmas Island as the best base for the tests, and by April 1957 this piece of coral (whose highest point was only 25 ft above sea level) boasted two runways, hardstandings and accommodation for a Task Group of 1300 men.

The Bomber Command element of the Task Group was to be responsible for the air drops, cloud sampling, high-level meteorological reconnaissance and cloud tracking, plus high-level PR of each burst. Canberras were to also rush cloud samples back to the UK. It was a firm requirement to obtain post-detonation samples from 'as great a height as is possible', and 'it is hoped to obtain the samples in the Canberra B 6 in the band 50,000 to 53,000 ft'. At the other extreme, the Canberra's mission was to reconnoitre ground zero from a height of 2000 ft within 15 minutes of detonation 'to assist with the immediate assessment of correct weapon functioning'.

The first live drop of a British thermonuclear weapon was made by Valiant XD818 on 15 May 1957, the bomber being captained by Wg Cdr Ken Hubbard. Ground zero for the burst was 400 miles south of Christmas Island near Malden Island. As he approached release at an altitude of 45,000 ft, Hubbard put XD818 into a slight dive. Immediately after release he rolled into a turn to port through 130 degrees at a constant measurement on the accelerometer of 1.7G at 0.76M. When Hubbard finally rolled out, and as the weapon detonated at 8000 ft, the slant range between XD818 and the air burst was 8.65 nautical miles. As the nuclear cloud mushroomed up behind them, the pilot of the No 100 Sqn Canberra photographing from a safe distance was heard to remark over the R/T, 'If you do that again, you'll have to marry me!'

Besides XD818 there were seven other aircraft airborne in the test area – a 'Grandstand' Valiant (to give crews experience of flash and blast from a thermonuclear weapon), five No 76 Sqn air sampler Canberra B 6s and a reconnaissance/meteorological Canberra PR 7 of No 100 Sqn. In the first B 6 the Sample Controller (Air), Air Cdre D A Wilson, assessed the heights and dimensions of the nuclear cloud and made the final decision, based

These Canberra B 6s of No 76 Sqn were photographed at their Weston Zoyland base in October 1956 on the eve of the unit's departure for Australia as part of the Montebello atomic test task force. No 76 Sqn was a specialist air-sampling unit whose jets supported Operations *Mosaic, Buffalo* and *Grapple* through to its disbandment in December 1960 (*Peter Green Collection*)

on radiation-measuring instruments, that it was safe for sampling aircraft to penetrate the cloud.

Secondly, a Radio Link and Target Reconnaissance B 6 was halfway between Christmas and Malden Islands in case of ground communications failure to and from the Joint Operations Centre. Once the Valiant was on the bombing run, this B 6 orbited 76 miles from the target, and just after release it began a maximum-rate descent towards Malden Island, levelling at 2000 ft. It then continued towards the target to see whether the bomb had in fact exploded at the correct altitude by looking for abnormal sea waves and fires on Malden Island, and by taking radiation measurements.

Then there was the Primary Sampler, which took off in time to arrive in the target area 30 minutes after the burst. Receiving the cloud's position from the Airborne Controller, it aimed to penetrate about an hour after the bomb burst. The crew took particulate and gaseous samples until the cumulative dose rate reached six Roentgens (the unit of measurement for ionising radiation). This B 6 carried limited fuel so that the aircraft could reach as high an altitude as possible. A Secondary Sampler followed the same profile 30 minutes later, and the fifth B 6 acted as Reserve Sampler in case the Primary or Secondary went unserviceable or later samples were needed – it was only used on the first *Grapple*.

Finally, in the lone PR 7, OC No 100 Sqn, Sqn Ldr Douggie Hammatt, with Flt Lt D Andrew as navigator, were responsible for weather reconnaissance and post-burst photography.

The first *Grapple* trial was a disappointment in that the 10,000-lb two-stage weapon exploded with a force of 300 KT rather than the predicted yield of about 1 MT. No 58 Sqn also lost Canberra PR 7 WH790 'during the final approach in inclement weather at RCAF Goose Bay, Labrador, on 16 May 1957, when Plt Off John Loomes and Flg Off T R "Monty" Montgomery sustained fatal injuries'. The PR 7 had apparently arrived over Goose Bay at 48,000 ft after a 4 hr 22 min flight from Namao, near Edmonton, Alberta. The crew, doubtless under pressure to get the precious samples back to the UK as quickly as possible, had had no proper sleep in the previous 26 hours and no proper meal for the previous 18 hours, and they made their airfield approach in very adverse weather conditions.

For No 100 Sqn navigator John Clubb, '8 November 1957 was one of the high points of my life so far, when, at precisely 1747 GMT, the equivalent of several million tons of high explosives went off about 25 miles away from where we were orbiting. This was the fourth airdropped *Grapple* bomb, and we were flying at 43,000 ft in a Canberra PR 7 in a predetermined orbit waiting to photograph the development of the nuclear fireball.

'Late in 1956, at Wyton, No 82 Sqn disbanded, and overnight its crews and Canberra PR 7 aircraft became the No 100 Sqn Reconnaissance Detachment. All crews were volunteers and the aircraft were extensively modified with navigation equipment (Green Satin, Ground Position Indicator and the Marconi Radio Compass) to help us to navigate over long stretches of water and over the United States, where we had to be able to fly airways using radio compass reporting points. Long-range high frequency voice radio equipment [HFRT] was also fitted to allow us to pass position reports and – our main role during the tests – weather information to the forecasters. We also had a side-facing camera for cloud (normal and nuclear) photography.

'We knew that "Sniff Boss" and "Sniffs 1, 2 and 3" were the Canberra B 6s that would fly through the cloud and obtain samples which courier Canberra PR 7s from our unit or No 58 Sqn would ferry back to the UK within 24 hours of the drop.

'On 8 November 1957, Brian Taylor and I were called to take over as last minute substitutes for "photo 1" – Sqn Ldr Monaghan and Flt Lt John Pomford – whose oxygen was running out much too quickly as they prepared to take up their orbit for the Valiant bomb run. We were airborne pretty quickly and just managed to climb to our operating height in time for a last minute drift and groundspeed check for the Valiant bomb-aimer, before taking up our orbit for post-burst photography.

'The tension as the Valiant started its live bomb run was like nothing I had felt before. To prevent flash blindness we faced away from ground zero just before the bomb left the Valiant, then closed our eyes and covered them with our hands as the bomb was falling and burst time approached. Despite these precautions, and the fact that my small window was fully covered by a curtain, it was impossible not to see the flash of the explosion 25 miles away as a brilliant white light – some people saw the bones of their hands as if x-rayed. After 20 or so more seconds the operations controller gave the order that we could open our eyes and look towards the explosion.

'I must say that when I saw the red and black fireball rising above its black stalk, before the characteristic white stalk and mushroom cloud developed, my first thought was that someone must have miscalculated and we would soon be heading north to Hawaii as Christmas Island would not be available for landing. My second thought, as I saw the dark concentric rings of blast waves coming up towards us, was that we wouldn't be flying at all after they had hit us. Then the training took over and we had to concentrate on taking the photographs as the fireball developed. As it happened, the scientists hadn't miscalculated, Christmas Island was undamaged. The blast waves just gave us a gentle nudge and we took some very good photographs. Six days later we were on our way back home.'

The reconnaissance detachment of No 100 Sqn was disbanded upon its return to Wyton in August 1957, with crews and aircraft being handed over to No 58 Sqn, which remained involved until the last *Grapple* test on 11 September 1958.

CANBERRA INTERDICTOR

The 1954 *Statement on Defence* noted 'we intend as soon as possible to build up in the RAF a force of medium bombers capable of using the atomic weapon to the fullest effect', adding 'atomic weapons are in production in this country and delivery to the forces has begun'. It was not until 1958 that the Canberras in Germany were given a nuclear capability, but it had long been clear that the high altitude unarmed jet bomber would eventually succumb to the surface-to-air missile. Mk 2 Vulcans and Victors would be provided with the Blue Steel stand-off missile, whereas salvation for the Canberra lay in operating at low-level.

Consequently, the RAF issued a requirement for a specialised Canberra interdictor optimised for low-level operations mainly at night behind enemy lines in visual contact with the ground using a variety of conventional bombs, guns and rockets. Based on the B 6, the B(I) 8 prototype (VX185) first flew on 23 July 1954 from Samlesbury. Overall fuselage length was the same as the B 6, but the most obvious new feature of the B(I) 8 was the extensively redesigned front fuselage.

The crew was reduced to two, and while the B(I) 8 pilot's ejection seat remained offset to port as in all other Canberras, he now sat under a fighter-style canopy to give increased visibility. The navigator's seat and

plotting table were moved forward into the B(I) 8's nose. He also had a second seat near the entry hatch for take-off and landing. Bizarrely, there was no ejection seat for the navigator on the B(I) 8. Equipped with a special flying suit with integrated parachute harness, the navigator was expected to find the parachute, clip it on, jettison the door and roll out of the stricken aircraft in the event of an emergency. A prone position was provided in the glazed nose for visual bomb aiming. The engines and most of the equipment in the B(I) 8 were the same as those in the B 6, and there was no significant difference in performance.

That said, the B(I) 8 was blessed with much improved armament. A detachable underwing pylon was fitted outboard of each engine, with each pod able to carry a 1000-lb bomb or 37 air-to-ground rockets. In addition, a gun pack with four 20 mm Hispano cannon could be fitted into the rear of the bomb-bay for use against ground targets – the aircraft carried a generous 525 rounds per gun. The forward bomb-bay held either three 1000-lb bombs or 16 flares for night attack, and the new fittings could be removed to restore the normal tactical bomb capability if required.

In addition, 22 B 6s were modified during assembly to undertake the interdictor role. These aircraft were fitted with the underwing pylons and bomb-bay gun pack of the B(I) 8, and were known as B(I) 6 Interim Interdictors.

The first production B(I) 8, WT326, flew on 8 June 1955, and the most natural place for the interdictors to be based, up close and personal in the event of any Warsaw Pact incursion, was RAF Germany. By the mid-1950s, the rapid rise to 24 Canberra bomber squadrons with ten aircraft each in the UK was causing headaches over where to base them, given the parallel programme to accommodate the new V-bombers. Brief consideration was given to upgrading Training Command airfields such as Worksop or Full Sutton, but in March 1954 a minute to CAS gave the reassuring advice that 'since the runways and taxiways are of the requisite Load Classification Number, we see no reason why four Canberra squadrons should not form at, say, Ahlhorn [in Germany], beginning 1 April this year'.

Canberra B 2s of No 35 Sqn are seen at Luqa during a deployment in 1958. The squadron's Pegasus crest can be seen adorning the aircrafts' tip tanks, and WJ635 also has the motif repeated on its fin. No 35 Sqn flew Canberras from April 1954 through to September 1961, when it disbanded in preparation for re-equipment with Vulcan B 2s (*Peter Green Collection*)

A three-ship formation of Canberra B 2s from No 27 Sqn perform a flypast over the Cypriot harbour town of Kyrenia during the unit's European tour in the summer of 1954. No 27 Sqn was equipped with Canberras from June 1953 through to December 1957, and it too would receive Vulcan B 2s in 1961 (*Peter Green Collection*)

A Tactical Development unit (TDU) had been formed at Ahlhorn on 23 February 1953 (with B 2s WH695, WH697, WH700 and WH701 fresh off the production line) to prove the Canberra in the night interdictor role. To assess the aircraft's vulnerability, the Nordhorn range was surrounded by searchlights and light ack-ack belonging to the British Army of the Rhine and the RAF Regiment. After the TDU's Canberras deployed to Brüggen, in Germany, on 24 July 1953 for airfield dispersal trials, the overall knowledge and expertise gained was fed into the final mock-up conference for the so-called 'New Look' interdiction Canberra.

On 29 March 1954 it was announced that four Canberra B 2 squadrons would form within the 2nd TAF. The first to arrive was No 149 Sqn, which took its ten B 2s from Cottesmore to Ahlhorn on 24 August 1954. The unit moved on to Gütersloh on 17 September to be followed by a newly re-formed No 102 Sqn on 20 October, No 103 Sqn on 30 November and No 104 Sqn on 15 March 1955. They were all assigned to No 551 Wing, which operated as any other Bomber Command B 2 wing, albeit positioned the furthest east. The jets' primary navigation and bombing aid was Gee-H, they flew at medium and high level, they dropped ordnance on both British and German ranges, they had the same crew classification system and they took part in the same exercises and competitions until all four Canberra B 2 squadrons disbanded as planned in August 1956.

The RAF Canberra force peaked at 34 squadrons in 1955, only for the total number to decline thereafter as V-bombers began to enter service. Four bomber units and one reconnaissance squadron gave up their Canberras in 1956, and ten UK-based squadrons were disbanded the following year.

The Canberra light bomber force in 1956 consisted of five B 6 and 19 B 2 squadrons, with a total Unit Establishment of 230 aircraft. These were equipped for visual bombing from heights of up to 43,000 ft, but their Gee-H radar bombing system was still described in a 1956 report to the Secretary of State as 'a ground-based aid liable to jamming'. This report referred to a chain of stations in northwest Europe extending to about 200 miles east of the Rhine, and provided seven days' warning could be obtained, plans existed to extend this coverage by positioning equipment at certain forward sites.

Additional navigational aids were Rebecca – fitted to all aircraft – and the radio compass, with which

Canberra B 2s of No 149 Sqn undergoing maintenance at Gütersloh in July 1956. The unit fin crest on WH713 was a horseshoe and a flash of lighting interlaced. Both aircraft also bears the No 551 Wing motif on their noses. No 149 Sqn disbanded on 31 August 1956 (*Peter Green Collection*)

A close up of the No 551 Wing motif on the nose of Canberra B 2 WD999, which was assigned to Sqn Ldr Shuster (OC No 103 Sqn) at Gütersloh. No 103 Sqn only operated Canberras from 30 November 1954 to 1 August 1956 (*Peter Green Collection*)

a small number of Canberras were fitted for operations overseas. Two B 6 squadrons were also equipped with the Blue Shadow sideways-looking search radar. None of the Canberras had any radio countermeasures equipment apart from Orange Putter. HQ Bomber Command stated in 1954 that Canberras were to be capable of carrying four automatic chaff dispensers in lieu of bombs, but nothing seemed to come of that.

Clive Elton carried on target marking with No 139 Sqn after the unit's return from Suez. 'We had Blue Shadow, which produced a roll of paper with radar traces on it. We used this to find the US Sixth Fleet on one occasion. We reported back, and the main bomber force went out to "destroy" the Fleet. Low-level target marking was antiquated by 1957, and we lost three crews in six months, but it was huge fun nevertheless. Target marking went out as nuclear weapons came in'.

NATO and UK strategy was being transformed from reliance on large conventional forces to smaller numbers of troops underpinned by nuclear deterrence. The RAF agreed to replace 162 Venoms in the 2nd TAF with 32 PR Canberras at Laarbruch, 48 B(I) 6/8 night interdictors and 48 Hunter day fighters. The Canberra interdictors would be based further back at Wildenrath, but they would pack a much bigger punch than the older B 2s. Once it became clear to the Americans that the UK was investing in a strategic nuclear capability, on 1 February 1957 the Eisenhower administration authorised the British CAS to discuss arrangements 'to furnish the RAF with US atomic bombs in the event of general war, and to coordinate the atomic strike plans of the USAF with the RAF'.

By 1953, the Atomic Weapons Research Establishment at Aldermaston, in Berkshire, had started development of new implosion concepts (air lenses) that would reduce the 10,000-lb Blue Danube to a 2000-lb weapon of the same yield, which could be carried internally by Canberras and externally by RAF and Royal Navy tactical strike aircraft. The first such weapon, known initially as the Javelin bomb and then Red Beard, was exploded over Australia in September 1956. A total of 142 Red Beard 10-15 KT nuclear weapons were acquired between October 1960 and May 1963, 48 of which were stored in Singapore (between 1961 and 1971) and 32 in Cyprus. Red Beard Mk 1 had significant limitations when stored at high temperature, so after November 1961 it was replaced by Red Beard Mk 2, which was better able to withstand life in Cyprus and Singapore.

A 1956 report from the VCAS said that the first Red Beard would be available to the RAF in late 1957. He added that English Electric was working on a full trial installation of an American weapon, and dropping trials from a partially modified Canberra were due to begin shortly at the Royal Aircraft Establishment. It was proposed to modify the B(I) 8 first, as the modification was simpler on this aircraft, thus providing 'an atomic capability in the shortest possible time'. The American nuclear weapon in question was the Mk 7 tactical atomic bomb, which weighed 1650 lbs and at 15 ft long could fit in the Canberra's bomb-bay.

By the end of 1959 the RAF had a national stockpile of only 71 fission bombs, and what was known as the Project 'E' arrangement would enable 168 US fission weapons to be operated on SACEUR-assigned Canberras as well as the V-force. The nuclear warheads remained under US custody,

Showing the flag – Canberra B 6s of No 139 'Jamaica' Sqn bask in the Caribbean sunshine at Kindley Field, Bermuda, in 1955 (*National Aerospace Library*)

and they were only for carriage in RAF aircraft in a general war. By 1963, British aircraft had access to 126 thermonuclear and 138 Red Beard operational warheads. This allowed the number of US Project 'E' gravity bombs stored for UK use to be reduced to 96, all of which were for tactical war fighting rather than deterrence in the bomb-bays of Canberras and Valiants assigned to the NATO land battle.

But a Canberra crew could not just drop a minimum of 8 KT (the Mk 7 had a variable yield) like any other free-fall bomb – the crew would have fried as they flew over the detonation. On 31 October 1956, an Air Ministry note informed the Head of Finance that 15 officers from squadrons, groups, HQ Bomber Command and the 2nd TAF had 'done a course under USAF instructors on loft and toss bombing, and on the qualities and handling of the Mk 7 weapon that is to be carried by the Canberra'. These officers 'constitute our instructors for the future', and the letter went on to say that groundcrew would begin training in handling and bombing-up techniques. It also noted that ML Aviation Ltd would be delivering bomb carriers to Maintenance Units, with the Aero 61B rack being 'the only item likely to give the show away'.

The 28 June 1957 edition of *Flight* magazine contained a review of the RAF's work and equipment. AVM Humphrey Edwardes Jones, C-in-C of the 2nd TAF, made no secret of the pressures his staff were facing as air units were re-disposed such that they became concentrated – with the exception of four Hunter squadrons at Jever and Gütersloh – between the Rhine and the Dutch and Belgian borders;

'One of the great difficulties is finding accommodation for squadron personnel at their new airfields. Where, say, three Hunter squadrons have been based with their generally younger [and probably unmarried] pilots, it may be difficult to find accommodation for two Canberra squadrons with double the number of crew members, probably of an older age group and having a larger proportion of married aircrew.'

Back in the UK, ACM Sir Harry Broadhurst, C-in-C Bomber Command, wrote that his 'mighty deterrent potential is there and ready to go at any hour of the day. Single V-bombers, or groups of them, can be deployed at a moment's notice. This applies also to the Canberra force, whose standards are no less high. Its role is, however, primarily to provide bomber support to SACEUR in case of a land attack on NATO countries. Reorganisation is now underway to concentrate these aircraft in No 1 Group, and to concentrate larger numbers of Canberras in a smaller number of squadrons as an administrative economy. A number of Canberra squadrons are also being re-equipped with V-bombers, and the aircraft so released are being used to re-equip squadrons already under the command of the Middle East and Far East Air Forces'.

The Canberra force was spreading its wings around the globe.

MIDDLE EAST AND FAR EAST

The Baghdad Pact of March 1955 was a defensive treaty of alliance 'for promoting shared political, military and economic goals' that was signed by Turkey, Iraq, the UK, Pakistan and Iran in March 1955. Iraq withdrew from the organisation in March 1959 following a coup, and the name of the Pact was duly changed to the Central Treaty Organisation (CENTO).

Initially, only the UK could provide a bomber element to the alliance, and by November 1955 there were plans for two Canberra B 2 squadrons – totalling 16 aircraft – to form within the MEAF. It was expected that they would eventually carry nuclear weapons, although 'a real nuclear potential' was not envisaged in the MEAF before 1959.

In May 1956 the UK Chiefs of Staff approved the assignment of four light bomber squadrons to the Baghdad Pact. During 1957, Venom-equipped Nos 32, 73, 6 and 249 Sqns in the MEAF and No 45 Sqn in the Far East Air Force (FEAF) received Canberra B 2s. The deployment of Nos 32 and 73 Sqns was mounted from Weston Zoyland, with the first two B 2s, WH870 and WK103 of No 32 Sqn, reaching Nicosia on 3 March 1957. The squadron completed its move from Nicosia to Akrotiri 16 days later. 'No clearly defined operational policy exists at the moment', said the No 32 Sqn ORB, 'but a preliminary directive from AHQ Levant [formerly Air Headquarters Iraq] lays down that crews are to become familiar with Middle Eastern air routes and attain a high standard of visual bombing as soon as possible. A shallow dive marker element is to be trained within the unit'. By April No 32 Sqn was equipped with eight aircraft.

No 73 Sqn flew out its first four aircraft from Weston Zoyland to Akrotiri over 19-20 March 1957, and another four followed ten days later. In its first month of operations from Akrotiri, the April ORB noted that flights to El Adem, Malta, Aden and Tehran 'gave experience to the crews of their operational area'.

The other two MEAF light bomber squadrons flew out from Coningsby in the summer and early autumn of 1957. No 6 Sqn arrived at Akrotiri in two flights – 'A' on 15 July and 'B' on 1 August. No 249 Sqn's departure from the UK was held up because its Venoms were out in Oman, preventing its groundcrews

Pakistani Air Force sentries guard a Canberra B 2 of No 73 Sqn at Mauripur air base on 6 April 1959. The unit's fin marking comprises a blue demi talbot with red maple leaf, all within a blue frame (*Peter Green Collection*)

Akrotiri-based Canberra B 15 WH947 of No 32 Sqn carries a single rocket pod beneath each wing. This aircraft, photographed circa 1964, was originally delivered to the RAF as a B 6 in October 1954. Following service with Nos 617 and 12 Sqns, as well as the Binbrook Wing, it was converted to B 15 specification and issued to No 32 Sqn in 1961. It remained with the Akrotiri Strike Wing until struck off charge in February 1968 (*No 32 Sqn via Andy Thomas*)

from getting back to Cyprus in time for the originally planned September arrival dates. Fog in Lincolnshire also delayed the unit's departure. No 249 Sqn eventually arrived at Akrotiri on 16 October, its two flights having left Coningsby on the same day, with a two-hour interval between them. Their arrival meant that Akrotiri now accommodated four Canberra bomber units, plus No 13 (PR) Sqn.

'The Middle East sphere of influence', wrote AM Sir Hubert Patch, C-in-C MEAF, in *Flight* on 28 June 1957, 'covers an area which stretches from Libya in the west to India in the east, and from the Caspian Sea to the northern tips of Mozambique and Madagascar. This vast domain, in which the MEAF plays a major part in support of British foreign policy, guards the right flank of NATO and is the gateway to the African Continent. The main focus of my Command is therefore the support of the Baghdad Pact, the maintenance of internal security in British colonies and protected territories and the safeguarding of the air and sea routes which run through the area'.

From his HQ at Episkopi, Sir Hubert was supported by two subordinate formations – AHQ Levant, based at Nicosia, and the Commander of British Forces in the Arabian Peninsula. In Sir Hubert's words, 'the forces in the northern group include light bomber squadrons capable of carrying nuclear weapons, high-speed photographic reconnaissance aircraft, long-range transport aircraft and interceptor fighters'. C-in-C MEAF's use of the word 'capable' is interesting because the Akrotiri Supplementary Storage Area that housed Red Beard was not 'taken over and occupied' until 28 September 1961. Simultaneously, Nos 32 and 73 Sqns re-equipped with the Canberra B 15 while No 249 Sqn began operating B 16s in October, followed by No 6 Sqn.

Essentially, Canberra B 15s and B 16s were B 6 conversions for service in the Middle and Far East. Both were designed to operate in the tactical nuclear or conventional bombing roles, or as ground attack aircraft. The normal internal 6000-lb bomb load was supplemented by provision for a folding-fin rocket pod under each wing. An F95 camera was incorporated in the nose, while a risible electric fan was fitted on the coaming for cockpit cooling. The B 16 was similar to the B 15, except for the Blue Shadow sideways-looking radar to enhance Nos 6 and 249 Sqns' target-marking responsibility.

It was not until late 1961 that the Akrotiri Canberra squadrons went nuclear. Known thereafter as the Strike Wing, these Canberra squadrons remained the nuclear backbone of CENTO until March 1969, when they were replaced by Vulcan B 2s of Nos 9 and 35 Sqns.

BLUE SHADOW VETERAN

Mike Knight flew Hastings and Comets before joining No 139 Sqn at Binbrook in 1958;

'We had Blue Shadow, and our Canberras were known as the B 6(BS). I was a "Marker Leader", with "Marker 1" and "2" plus "Flare 1" and "2" leading the main bomber force. How did we target mark? We relied on decent navigators, trained in the old-fashioned way, with the assistance – when working to spec – of Blue Shadow radar. I guess there was the usual element of luck involved, combined of course with some superb piloting skills!

'Once in the target area those "x" million candlepower flares worked surprisingly well, but the onus for final guidance of the main force rested firmly with "Marker 1", and that was done visually. We would drop the flares ourselves and then dive underneath to circle the target and lay target indicators at about 300-500 ft AGL [above ground level], hoping all the while to dodge the bombs. We gave instructions to the main force like "bomb into easterly greens". Crazy, really, but it all seemed rather good fun at the time.

'I recall a very sad occasion at El Adem when one of the squadron's flight commanders followed his TIs into the ground and, with ghoulish black humour, the cry went out "bomb into the burning Canberra".'

The Binbrook wing disbanded during 1959, and Mike Knight led four selected target-marking crews to Cyprus, where they joined No 249 Sqn – the combination being colloquially known as 'No 12349 Sqn'. In his words, 'we became part of the Akrotiri Strike Wing, with nuclear and conventional roles within CENTO. On 30 June 1961, my crew was sent to do a recce in Tehran prior to leading a Javelin detachment to the Far East. At 2 am, whilst in a night club drinking vodka tonic – vodka in a coffee pot and tonic in a milk jug because the Shah decreed no alcohol – we received a signal via the Embassy to "return Akrotiri soonest". We could only fly over Turkish airspace during daylight, so we crossed the Turkish border as dawn broke. We were ordered to bomb up in response to a possible Iraq invasion of Kuwait'.

An RAF Germany Canberra B(I) 8 strike squadron was brought into Sharjah, in the United Arab Emirates, to help deter Iraqi designs on Kuwait. But unlike Operation *Desert Storm* 30 years later, C-in-C Middle East Command (AM Sir Charles Elworthy) could not obtain clear guidance on the extent to which he could use his Canberra striking force for counter-offensive action against Iraqi forces in the rear area between Basra and the Kuwait frontier. That said, it was made clear that should the Iraqi Air Force attack any Kuwaiti target, it would immediately bring retaliation from Canberras in the Persian Gulf and Cyprus. Whenever concern about Kuwait resurfaced, as at the end of 1964, No 13 Sqn PR Canberras would plot the position of Iraqi armour almost on a daily basis.

Canberra B 2s (WJ609 of No 21 Sqn in the foreground) at Khormaksar, Aden, along with local camel-mounted troops, in March 1955 (*Peter Green Collection*)

During 1964 a series of detachments to Sharjah was made by six B 15s and B 16s from Cyprus, partly to boost the number of RAF aircraft in the skies over Oman, but also to keep the Canberra wing up to speed with live firing on the Rashid Range. At other times PR Canberras would reconnoitre during Saudi Arabian border disputes or to survey the more remote parts of Oman.

Mike Knight was given command of No 32 Sqn in 1961, and on Boxing Day that year 'we were ordered to make a no-notice transit to El Adem, en route for Nairobi, where we were held for a few weeks in preparation for operations to counter one of the periodic Iraqi threats to Kuwait. We were armed with a less than awe-inspiring load of six 1000-lb "dumb" bombs and 74 2-in high-explosive [HE] rocket projectiles – 37 in each of two pods. After a couple of weeks on standby, we were recalled to Cyprus.

'This Nairobi caper gave pause for thought – not least because the RPs had been delivered to us with little more information than the Microcell brochure on "carriage and release". My PAI [Pilot Attack Instructor] was the irrepressible "Manx" Kelly, and he took it upon himself to solve the problem. We had a number of discussions – all of which pointed to the obvious conclusion that the only way to use these little beauties was to go in as low and as fast as the old Canberra could manage. At the time we were considering not just aircraft on the ground as targets but also the 'catalytic crackers' of Iraqi oilfields, which, if successfully attacked, might just get up the nose of their comparatively new leader. Whether or not such a venture was likely to be effective was hardly the point. We felt distinctly short of viable options.

'We set up the first trials which, from memory, "Manx" had calculated as a minimum 300-knot approach at precisely 67 ft AGL. In the event, experience gave us the confidence to increase the former and reduce the latter.

'I was designated to lead this trial and, to keep everyone sweet, I asked that a crew from each of the B 15/16 squadrons be unofficially detached to the enterprise. I was delighted to welcome David Lloyd from No 6 Sqn, "Boz" Robinson from No 73 Sqn and "Curly" Hirst from No 249 Sqn. Together with my own crew, and that of "Manx" Kelly, I felt we had more than enough clout to get results. Galling as it was to these fine pilots, I insisted on the need for screen rides with their new leader, and these were flown on 15 July 1963 in the order Hirst/Lloyd/Robinson/Kelly, initially at 100 ft AGL.

'We were well aware of the propensity of the odd one of these little rockets to fly in a rather eccentric manner, and there were one or two quite exciting moments. I recall that both pods discharged reasonably straight ahead, covering a vast area out to sea, though with minimal assessment of accuracy on target – the hessian screens that were mounted on the foreshore faired rather ill from the onslaught.

'Our CENTO nuclear role involved last minute loading and target study. We had targets in the southern USSR, which were regarded as "one-way tickets". We flew constituted crews, with the standard Combat and Combat Star classifications.'

In early February 1963, 'Boz' Robinson joined No 73 Sqn in Cyprus; 'As part of our wide-ranging troubleshooting role, the unit took part in an exercise in Kenya, and I was able to persuade my CO, Colin Foale –

the father of Britain's first astronaut – that he might find an experienced ground-attack pilot of value since the Canberras were to provide air support to the land force. I duly found myself attached to 70 Brigade, King's African Rifles, whose Brigadier was Fitzalan-Howard, later Duke of Norfolk. My job was to advise him on when and where to make use of No 73 Sqn crews, with their capability to deliver 74 2-in rockets in a shallow dive, or to drop six 1000-lb bombs from level flight.

'The crew of a B 15 constituted a single pilot supported by a navigator sitting in the left side ejection seat behind the pilot, and a navigator/observer in the right hand bang seat. His job was to move either down into the nose to carry out level bombing runs or to sit alongside the pilot in the Rumbold seat to affect a better lookout to the starboard side when combat became imminent. Travelling on the Rumbold seat was no great hardship – many a staff officer has been grateful for that mode of transport in an emergency, and many an "erk" has been equally content to travel thus to reach a sick relative. The Canberra, when not carrying bombs, could be used as a convenient transporter. Fitted with two large panniers in the bomb-bay, the aircraft could be used to move fruit, vegetables, milk and a variety of other goods around the Middle East during everyday navigation exercises.

'My two navigators had come straight from training. At Bassingbourn they had chosen me as their pilot because I had some 2000 hours [of] experience already, but I was not making too good an impression among the dyed-in-the-wool bomber pilots on No 73 Sqn who composed the majority of the Strike Wing. They were not keen to have their ideas about bombing tactics questioned by a young upstart from Fighter Command. No Sir!

'Our supposed targets in times of tension were Syrian Air Force airfields, and to destroy their aircraft before they could get airborne meant a surprise low-level attack using rocket projectiles. These were tactics that the predominantly "bomber" guys at Akrotiri had never trained for, and we had to bring everyone into the picture so they could operate at very low levels with confidence.

'Under the guidance of the very positive and gung-ho Mike Knight, "Manx" Kelly, "Curly" Hirst and I began rocket delivery trials and later converted the wing pilots to low-level rocket delivery. This was a method of attacking parked aircraft by surprise and approaching at a speed of 300 knots and a height of only 35 ft AGL using the normally reliable radar altimeter. That was really fast and low, and quite exciting!

Canberra B 16 WJ778 of No 249 Sqn is refuelled in Bahrain during a deployment from Cyprus. The elephant crest beneath the Akrotiri Strike Wing badge emphasised the squadron's wartime association with the Gold Coast. No 249 Sqn flew the B 16 from October 1962 until the unit's disbandment in February 1969 (*Peter Green Collection*)

'We began the trials by running in toward the target at Larnaca Range [now Larnaca Airport] at a height of 60 ft AGL, moving down to 35 ft later when people felt happy at 60 ft. Height was checked using the radar altimeter, and when the pipper in the centre of the gunsight ran on to the target at a range of 1000 yards in absolutely level flight the pilot pressed the firing button. The rockets devastated the target and a 4g escape manoeuvre ensured that the aircraft flew well clear of any ricocheting rockets or debris. Well, that was the theory!

'Although this method generally worked well, problems were encountered with "twirlers" – rockets that instead of following a direct path to the target malfunctioned in some way and took a zigzag path into the ground much closer than 1000 yards! They sometimes threw up debris or ricocheted directly into the path of the aircraft, resulting in the pilot having to perform exciting evasive manoeuvres. The process of getting all the wing pilots qualified at low-level RP delivery went on for almost a year.

'In Cyprus, our flying pattern was to start with a met briefing at 0700 hrs in the air-conditioned operations block, then to disperse to the outlying squadron buildings scattered about the eastern end of the airfield. After passing No 249 Sqn's place, you could turn right for No 32 Sqn or left for No 73 Sqn. Beyond lay No 13 Sqn, with its PR 9s. No 6 Sqn was the odd man out by being situated at the western end of the field, more than a mile away from us and quite close to the transport aircraft dispersals and the helicopter zone.

'Early in the morning the temperature seemed quite pleasant, but by lunchtime going into the operations block felt like entering a fridge because the outside temperature would be around 30°C. Our Canberra B 15s and B 16s did not have the opening canopy that the PR 9 had, so our groundcrew would station an air-conditioner just outside the side door and put a large umbrella over the top of the cockpit some time before the crew arrived to conduct their pre-flight checks. Although this arrangement gave the aircrew a reasonably comfortable start to a trip, once the door had to be closed to start the engines, the cool air supply was cut off and the umbrella removed. Then the temperature inside the cabin became very hot very quickly. We had a simple rule that if it became impossible to get into the air within seven minutes of shutting the door then the pilot could abort the sortie.'

It was decided that the Canberra should be fitted with a guided air-to-surface missile fitted on an additional pylon mounted outboard of the existing one. What was chosen was the French Nord AS.30, which was controlled in flight visually via a small joystick. The AS.30 was a big weapon – it weighed 520 kg, with a 240-kg impact-fused semi-armour piercing HE warhead – and it needed a Canberra to carry it. The missile's SFOM 83A sighting device was fitted in the bomb-aimer's position. No 73 Sqn was the first to introduce the AS.30 into service, spending most of 1965 working up on the system before conducting its first live firings in November. No 32 Sqn was next to get the missile.

Akrotiri Canberras also provided fighter affiliation targets for CENTO air forces to pit their wits against. Lightning F 3s from No 56 Sqn, Turkish F-100 Super Sabres and Iranian F-4s were all routinely exercised with, and 'Boz' Robinson also deployed to Pakistan in May 1963 to provide practice intercept training for the Pakistani Air Force (PAF);

'The PAF requested that we remain below 40,000 ft, but when the Canberra had used up half of its fuel it could be cruise-climbed much higher. As a fighter pilot I thought it would be a good idea to even the score a little and, despite the briefing, climbed with my No 2, Dave Willis, toward 48,000 ft. My navigators were working hard, one keeping us on track, the other helping me with lookout to spot the incoming fighters. Suddenly, I saw two F-104s way below the left wing, and without any hope of carrying out an intercept on us. In those days there was no air-to-air missile threat from those F-104s, so their only chance of a kill would have been from a guns attack.

Canberra B 15 WH955 of No 32 Sqn cruises over the Himalayas. The Akrotiri-based unit periodically flew across the Indian subcontinent when travelling to and from Tengah, in Singapore ('Boz' Robinson)

'I decided to play a game and hard turned into the F-104s. Too late I remembered that the 100 series Avons fitted to the Canberra didn't like that sort of treatment. There were two loud pops and then silence! I had flamed out both engines and would now have to descend to below 20,000 ft to relight them. News of our escapade in northern Pakistan, coupled with the loss of a No 6 Sqn B 16 and its crew of three caught in a cumulo-nimbus in the vicinity of Khartoum, convinced my colleagues that the 100 series Avon required careful handling above 40,000 ft.

'We spent much of our times as a crew doing nuclear target study. Our target was a large city on the west coast of the Caspian Sea inside the Soviet Union – a place I visited in my later role as British air attaché in Moscow. After so many years, it is hard to remember exactly one's feelings about being a nuclear bomber. I don't think we lost much sleep over the fact.'

By the summer of 1965, Akrotiri Canberras were back at Sharjah for weapons practice on the Gulf ranges and low-level navigation exercises over the featureless desert. Weeks were spent on intensive shallow dive-bombing, getting ready for action even further east – an operational role in Malaya.

THE FAR EAST

The very first Canberra to drop bombs in anger was a No 101 Sqn B 6 that had deployed to Malaya in 1955 as part of Operation *Firedog*. Since 1948 the RAF had been battling Communist insurgents in Malaya with a variety of piston-engined aircraft, including Lincolns.

No 101 Sqn was the first RAF jet bomber squadron to be selected for active duty overseas, and four B 6s duly took off from Binbrook for Changi on 7 February 1955. Led by Sqn Ldr W D Robertson, the B 6s moved forward to Butterworth for Canberra tropical trials, bombing insurgents in their jungle hideouts during the course of the deployment. Hitting roughly constructed bashas under dense jungle foliage with 1000-lb bombs as directed by Air Observation Post Austers, or against a six-figure map reference provided by a ground liaison officer, was asking a lot. On one occasion No 101 Sqn overshot the aiming datum by 3000 yards.

During four-and-a-half months, No 101 Sqn carried out 98 operational sorties, of which 43 were on pinpoint and 55 on area

Canberra B 6s of No 12 Sqn in 1958. The unit undertook a five-month deployment to Butterworth between October 1955 and March 1956 in support of the FEAF's commitment to the Malayan Emergency (*Peter Green Collection*)

Canberra B 2 WH853 'D-Dog' of No 45 Sqn drops a salvo of 1000-lb bombs during anti-terrorist operations in Malaya. The unit saw extensive operational service in the Far East whilst based in Singapore as the resident FEAF strike squadron. WH853 was the first production B 2 built by Short Bros of Belfast, being initially assigned to No 10 Sqn in January 1953. It was lost in a fatal accident on 18 November 1958 when the jet stalled on take-off from Tengah after suffering double engine failure and hit trees and crashed into Kranji Creek north of the airfield. The pilot and one of two navigators onboard perished (*Peter Green Collection*)

targets. The remainder of 1955 saw successive deployments by six or eight B 6s from Nos 617 and 12 Sqns, and in March 1956 No 9 Sqn deployed to Butterworth with eight aircraft. These detachments were known as Operation *Mileage*.

As the official historian of the Malayan Emergency put it, 'Canberras carried half the bomb load of Lincolns and their cruising speed of 250 knots at the optimum bombing height required more elaborate navigational aids and made map-reading impracticable and visual bomb-aiming difficult. The pilot had a poorer visibility than in a Lincoln and the Canberra could not be flown at night or in close formation, and could not be employed in a strafing role. They suffered, in common with all jet aircraft in the tropics, from a serious limitation in their endurance at low level, which precluded postponing or delaying an air strike once they were airborne. This was a serious disadvantage in the uncertain weather conditions of Malaya, especially when Canberras were operating in the northern part of the country far from their parent base at Tengah, Singapore'.

There were two resident RAF strike units in Malaya in 1956, namely Nos 45 and 60 Sqns, both equipped with Venoms. No 45 Sqn started working up on Canberra B 2s from November 1957, followed during 1958 by Nos 2(B) RAAF and 75 RNZAF Sqns, also with Canberra B 2s. Re-equipment of No 45 Sqn was completed with the arrival of its second Canberra flight at Tengah on 9 January 1958, but its B 2s were not used in *Firedog* operations until 18 March, when the first strike by in-house FEAF Canberras – Operation *Ginger* – saw four aircraft drop six 500 pounders. They made their final *Firedog* strike in August 1959. Looking back, Euro-centric Canberras were too elaborate for the counter-insurgency task in Malaya.

No 81 Sqn with its Meteor PR 10s bore the brunt of the photo-reconnaissance commitment throughout the Malayan Emergency, although periodic assistance was forthcoming when four PR 7s of No 542

Sqn arrived at Changi in May 1955. These aircraft were replaced at three-monthly intervals by similar detachments (reducing to two aircraft as of 14 June 1956) from Nos 540, 82 and 58 Sqns. These ceased as a regular commitment in October 1956, but Bomber Command continued to provide two PR Canberras to the FEAF for two-month periods twice a year, usually from January to March and from July to September, for the remainder of the Emergency.

No 81 Sqn re-equipped with Canberra PR 7s from February 1960. In early 1962 the unit was engaged in surveying the Thai border from where it joined the Burmese border in the west through the Laotian segment in the north to the Cambodian border in the east. Meanwhile, No 45 Sqn soldiered on with rather tired B 2s flying at low level until the first B 15 arrived at Tengah in August 1962. No 45 Sqn's last pair of B 2s (by then the only operational B 2 bombers left in the RAF) were flown back to the UK in December. Jeff Jefford joined No 45 Sqn as a navigator in August 1962;

'The B 15s were warmed over B 6s, which meant an extra 1000 lbs of thrust per side, with the luxury of a three-shot starting capability in place of the B 2's single cartridge, and integral wing tanks so we could do Hong Kong direct without having to stage through Clark AFB in the Philippines.

'The most significant difference was the major increase in operational flexibility conferred by the B 15's avionics fit and its range of weapon options. The Air Position Indicator had been replaced by a Ground Position Indicator driven by a Blue Silk Doppler radar, which provided a reasonably accurate and self-contained means of navigation. A radio altimeter was another addition – potentially useful over open country, but questionable over dense jungle because you could never be sure if the signals were bouncing off the forest floor or the tops of trees. In addition to the original VHF radio, we now had UHF and HF.

'The ability to carry six 1000-lb bombs internally was unimpaired, but the new variant also had a pylon under each wing, and they could take another 1000 pounder each. In practice the squadron never exercised this option, although later on the pylons were used to carry 25-lb practice bombs when toss-bombing was added to the attack options. Alternatively, each pylon could be fitted with a Microcell pod containing 37 2-in RPs, giving the potential to fire a salvo of up to 74 which, since this did not interfere with the ability to carry bombs in the bomb-bay, provided the aircraft with a quite respectable ground attack capability.'

The gunsights arrived in February 1963 and Pilot Attack Instructor Neville Whittaker immediately started checking out the pilots in RP techniques, initially using a 20-degree dive attack and firing at 1500 yards.

Hunter FGA 9s of No 20 Sqn arrived at Tengah in late 1961, and it was decided to operate them together with the B 15s in what was known as the Offensive Support Wing.

Canberra B 15 WH948 of No 45 Sqn conducts one of the last bombing sorties for the unit with the aircraft in December 1969. All the Canberras went when the squadron disbanded in February 1970. Dark Green and Dark Sea Grey camouflage with silver undersides (replaced by Light Aircraft Grey) had been introduced to No 45 Sqn Canberras from 1964 (*Peter Green Collection*)

There were seven B 15s at Tengah by 8 December 1962 when Sheikh Azahari launched a revolution in Brunei. The first No 81 Sqn PR 7 sortie in response to this emergency was flown by Robin Brown, with Steve Armstrong as navigator. This was a low-level photo-reconnaissance mission undertaken in pretty appalling weather, and they struck an unmarked aerial mast, which tore some seven to eight feet off a wingtip. Robin managed to coax the aircraft safely back to Labuan some 30 miles away. On 10 December, WH969 from No 45 Sqn, flown by Jeff Thomas and Don Sleven, and accompanied by Ian Pedder (OC Offensive Support Wing), carried out a reconnaissance of the Seria-Anduki area. The rebels were talking to the Shell representatives at Seria by telephone and threatening to use hostages as a shield in an attack on the police post at Panaga. At that point the Canberra B 15 roared overhead. A new voice promptly came on the line and promised that the hostages would come to no harm.

The last of the original batch of B 15s, WH958, arrived at Tengah on 13 January 1963, having flown direct from Delhi. A great deal of weapons training was carried out over the Song Song Range, with most crews flying double sorties and dropping a total of 16 bombs. After a low-level cross-country to the range to drop the first eight, they would land at Butterworth, grab a steak sandwich and a Coke in No 2(B) Sqn's crewroom, move the spare eight bombs forward to the live carriers and repeat the sortie in reverse to land back at Tengah.

In October 1963 No 45 Sqn began to train with the Low Altitude Bombing System (LABS). In Jeff Jefford's words, 'LABS was yet another approach to the problem of low-level bombing, particularly in the context of delivering Red Beard and getting away with it. The introduction of LABS complicated training as crews were now required to be proficient in this technique, as well as conventional low-level and high-level bombing, RP attacks and high and low-level navigation. This was a much wider range of activities than had been required a year before, and the problem was exacerbated by the need for slightly different aircraft fits to execute some of these roles.

'With one aeroplane usually away on a Ranger or a Borneo run, there were rarely more than four Canberras available for routine training, and this was insufficient to provide the necessary flexibility to permit crews to do what they liked when they liked. To manage this problem the squadron tended to operate at high level for a couple of weeks, then spend a fortnight on intensive RP work, then a period of LABS and so on. This way a crew would be pretty good at what it was presently doing, and it ought to have be no more than about six weeks since it had had a go at everything else. This arrangement was a very satisfactory compromise, and the cyclic approach to training remained in vogue until 1970.'

In the months leading up to the creation of the state of Malaysia,

A 50th birthday grouping of No 45 Sqn Canberras at Tengah in 1966, including a natural metal T 4 (*via Jefford*)

President Sukarno of Indonesia began to promote what came to be known as 'Confrontation' – a state of armed political and economic hostility, sometimes including direct military involvement, but stopping short of outright war. From mid-1963, bands of guerrillas made incursions across the border from Kalimantan, and the possibility of a direct attack could not be ruled out. While the army established forward posts in Borneo and began patrolling the border, it was decided to assess Kuantan, in Pahang, as a dispersal airfield. No 45 Sqn mounted Exercise *Merrydown* between 2 and 8 October 1963 – a full-scale deployment to Kuantan with all eight of its B 15s, which proved that it was perfectly feasible to operate a light bomber squadron from this relatively primitive site.

Aerial sharp end during Confrontation – a No 45 Sqn Canberra B 15 leading a Javelin FAW 9 of No 64 Sqn and a Hunter FGA 9 of No 20 Sqn. Once Confrontation got serious in mid-1964, the big white serials were painted over in black and the big white discs on the fins of the Canberras were replaced by jaunty little camels on the fin and the nose. Before the year was out the big black serials had also been replaced – by little ones in black (*via Jefford*)

Using four Canberras and two four-ships of Hunters during the summer of 1964, a typical Offensive Support Wing strike involved the B 15s plastering the area with a barrage of 296 2-in RPs followed by the two sections of Hunters with their heavier 60-lb rockets. As the last of these cleared the area, the Canberras ran back in to drop 24,000 lbs of bombs and the Hunters then returned to rake the target with cannon fire. It was tried out with considerable success during Exercise *Raven* on the inland range at Asahan on 19 July.

On 17 August about 100 Indonesian regulars were landed by boat near Pontian, on the west coast of Johore, and as Indonesian airspace was only 15 miles south of Tengah, a low-level surprise air attack could not be discounted. The FEAF had had a virtually permanent detachment of V-bombers since December 1963. Gordon Gilbert was CO of No 81 Sqn, and he recalled that on 12 September 'a very welcome reinforcement by two PR 9s and crews from No 58 Sqn, led by flight commander Tony Vasey, arrived from Wyton. This was the first of a succession of detachments provided on rotation from the UK and Malta for the duration of Confrontation, including a pair of PR 9s'. No 73 Sqn B 15s came in from Akrotiri and a composite squadron of B(I) 8s prepared to deploy from Germany.

A general state of emergency was declared in mid-September, and No 45 Sqn was ordered to exercise its dispersal option. On 17 September all eight of the squadron's bombers, half of them loaded with 1000 pounders and the others with RPs, their crews being issued with sidearms, deployed to Kuantan. The unit returned to Singapore on 9 October, their place at Kuantan being taken by the composite squadron of Canberra B(I) 8s that had finally arrived from Germany. From 19 October No 45 Sqn spent several days on standby at a very high state of readiness but nothing dramatic happened.

At the end of 1964 a group of Indonesian troops landed off the southwestern tip of Johore, and Operation *Birdsong* was mounted to dislodge them. This consisted of simulated strikes by Hunters and Canberras on 23 and 24 December, but the Indonesians refused to give themselves up. On Boxing Day, OC No 45 Sqn (Brian Carruthers) and his crew, assisted by an airborne forward air controller (FAC) in a Whirlwind helicopter, loosed off live rockets, which did the trick. It was to be the last live offensive sortie flown by an RAF Canberra.

Canberra bomber reinforcement of the FEAF during Confrontation was as follows;

Who	When	Where
No 73 Sqn	9-11/64	Tengah
Nos 3/14 Sqns	10-11/64	Kuantan
No 32 Sqn	11/64 to 2/65	Tengah
No 16 Sqn	2-6/65	Kuantan
No 249 Sqn	6-8/65	Kuantan
No 6 Sqn	8-9/65	Kuantan
No 73 Sqn	9-11/65	Kuantan
No 32 Sqn	11-12/65	Kuantan

No 45 Sqn Canberra crews settled into a routine at Labuan, where an Air Weapons Range was laid out at Balembangan Island, off the northernmost tip of Sabah, to allow pop-up bombing training to continue. Variety was provided by the continuing requirement to fly border patrols, while No 45 Sqn would also undertake Operations *Monomania* and *Tennon* from Kai Tak in 1965, 1966 and 1967 to 'sniff' Chinese nuclear tests, using B 6s provided for that purpose.

There were training detachments with US tactical fighter squadrons and, towards the end of September 1965, No 45 Sqn cooperated with No 205 Sqn on Exercise *Shaving Brush* to test the feasibility of bombing and rocket attacks at night by the light of flares dropped from Shackletons. It worked, and the trials were extended into October to refine the techniques. The bulk of No 45 Sqn had been back from Labuan since June, leaving one Canberra at the disposal of the Borneo ground commander. This commitment changed in October, with three aeroplanes being detached to Kuching, but on weekends only. Indonesian interest in Confrontation was waning fast, and the last Canberra detachment returned to Tengah on 8 November. From then on No 45 Sqn was required to do no more than respond if the commitment were to be reinstated. As tension relaxed, No 32 Sqn was not replaced when it flew back to Cyprus in December 1965.

Jeff Jefford described what the FEAF bombers were supposedly going to do in event of full-scale war in the region;

'The B 15 was nuclear capable and No 45 Sqn's crews maintained currency with LABS but, as a very junior flying officer, no one ever saw

Canberra B 15s of No 45 Sqn at Tengah in 1963, each jet being meticulously marked with large white serial numbers and the prominent fin motif (a red flying camel with blue wings on a white disc). As noted in the previous caption, these had all gone by the end of 1964 (*Peter Green Collection*)

fit to tell *me* why. We surely weren't going to "nuke" Djakarta, so I imagine that there must have been some sort of plan for "doing it" to China. I have a vague recollection that there may have been some highly classified stuff relating to China held in the Ops Block vault, but I was never given access to any of *that*. What we did have squirreled away in the vault was a selection of mission folders, which we drew up ourselves, for various conventional targets in Indonesia. My personal war plan involved an attack, so far as I was aware, by just *one* Canberra on Djakarta airport, after which we were to recover to Labuan. Here, we were to rearm, refuel and do it again on the way home after lunch, this time attacking a target at Pontianak, in Kalimantan [southern Borneo].'

'Boz' Robinson, detached from Akrotiri with No 73 Sqn, remembered that 'off the coast of Malaya at Kuantan from a height of 5000 ft one could look down and see the ghostly shapes of the *Prince of Wales* and *Repulse* lying about five nautical miles offshore.

'Our targets were Indonesian airfields, where their aircraft were dispersed. My target was Djakarta airport, which had both civil and military aircraft, and we did not wish to inflict damage on the civil guys. After much deliberation we agreed that I would lead six aircraft at very low level – 50 ft or lower – and my wingman and I would employ 148 2-in rocket projectiles against the lined-up MiGs and Tupolevs. Thereafter, while the other four aircraft did the same thing, but from different angles, we [the first pair] would pull up to 6000 ft in a continuous climbing turn and roll in for a 30-degree dive attack against the same aircraft, or others that became visible during the course of the manoeuvre, before descending back down to 50 ft to make our getaway. The other two pairs would do the same. We would have delivered 444 2-in rockets and 36 1000-lb bombs to make President Sukarno's eyes water.

'The nearest we on No 73 Sqn got to flying this mission was to be brought to two minutes readiness, which lasted for about six hours. That certainly concentrated the mind!'

Above and around the strike action flew the Canberra PR 7s of No 81 Sqn. 'Hally' Hardie was a first tour navigator who arrived on No 81 Sqn as the last few PR 7s were being delivered in 1962. 'We had two significant roles', he recalled, 'intelligence work across the other side during Confrontation and the on-going survey of Borneo to update maps.

'Over Indonesia we generally used a fan of F52 36-in or F52 24-in cameras, backed up the F49 survey camera. The F52 48-in oblique camera was used to photograph Indonesian airfields. We used the periscope through the sextant mounting to check we weren't trailing, and we were never intercepted. It might have been different if the Indonesians had made their MiG-21s serviceable.

'Deep penetration trips over Indonesia were authorised directly from Downing Street, so we were told. On one of these over Balikpapan, southern Kalimantan, MiG-17s and MiG-19s were flying circuits as we photographed from around 32,000-33,000 ft. We presumed they were not aware of our presence. Other interesting No 81 Sqn

The Microcell 2-in rocket pod was routinely carried by the 39 Canberra B 15s and 19 B 16s serving with the RAF. Each pod carried 37 rockets (*via Jefford*)

A No 81 Sqn Canberra PR 7 is seen on final approach to Kai Tak airport in Hong Kong during the 1960s. Although based at Tengah, the unit sent its photo-reconnaissance Canberras all over Southeast Asia and Oceana (*Alan Harrison*)

tasks included a sneak at the Paracels in 1963 and another sneak at the Maldives capital of Male in 1964 during a period of suspect activity by the then ruler.

'The aerial survey of Borneo had been underway for years because much of the rainforest covering the high ground of the interior was almost permanently shrouded in cloud. The weather was appalling. We never got rid of the cloud unless a typhoon dragged it off. There was only a short window of opportunity when we got the right amount of shadow for useful survey photography.'

In February 1965 two PR 7s, with groundcrew support, deployed to RAAF Darwin for an air defence exercise known as *Hot Squirrel*. Notwithstanding the demands of Confrontation, No 81 Sqn's Canberras were also involved in night low-level photography during Exercise *Air Boon Choo* over Thailand and the remnants of *Firedog* coverage over northeast Malaysia.

Alan Harrison had completed one PR Canberra tour with No 31 Sqn in Germany before being posted to No 81 Sqn towards the end of 1968. 'After the tense regime of the 2nd ATAF in Germany, with constant alerts and flying low-level in all weathers, it was a very pleasant change to be on No 81 Sqn, with the mix of high- and low-level flying and many detachments. During my 14 months on the squadron I went to Gan, in the Maldives, Malaya, Borneo, Hong Kong, New Zealand, Australia, the Cocos Keeling Islands, Bali and Djakarta.

'There were some differences flying in the FEAF. We had to have coolers in the cockpit before and during start-up, and once off the ground we immediately climbed to 20,000 ft to cool down! We also had to contend with the thunderstorms. The squadron was still trying to complete the survey of Borneo, and when we eventually finished it, the Malay Mapping Office produced the first two quarter-million scale maps, which they proudly came to show us. Unfortunately, as the Nav Leader pointed out, they did not abut with one another, and in the gap between them was Mount Kinabalu, the highest mountain in Southeast Asia!'

When Confrontation was over, No 81 Sqn was invited by the Indonesians to extend the Borneo survey to include Kalimantan. In 1969, all the maps had on them was a coast line, and in one navigator's words, 'we would pick a spot on the coast, fly inland for 200 miles with the F49 survey camera clicking away in the rear camera bay, execute a 180-degree turn and fly back to the coast with the satisfaction that we had taken the first survey photographs of this part of the world. This was carried out at 20,000 ft. Somewhat higher, with a minimum altitude of 50,000 ft, was the "job" in Hong Kong. This was flown with an F52 oblique with a 48-in lens in the front camera bay, which could record objects out to 60 miles. We were given a track to fly over the ground and points to switch the camera on and off. On landing, the film was whisked away and, although we had exposed it, we were not allowed to see the results'.

During the Kalimantan survey, the Indonesian defence attaché would put his seal on the back of the magazine fitted to the F49 camera prior to the mission being flown, and on landing back at Tengah he would check to make sure that the seal was still intact. He would then accompany the magazine to the processing laboratory and eventually depart with prints. There were no such restrictions placed on the PR 7's two F52s fitted in the nose, however, the groundcrew opening the front hatch and taking the magazines for processing. Aircrew involved in these flights had been briefed to photograph anything of interest that was seen while surveying Indonesian territory.

Alan Harrison's 'most interesting moment came while climbing out of RAAF Butterworth in northern Malaya. We were told to hold at 20,000 ft as an Australian Mirage had been hit by lightning, and they were trying to recover the jet. Unfortunately, we were in the middle of a thunderstorm. The aircraft was going up and down like an express lift and the noise from the hailstones was so great that the pilot and I could not communicate over the intercom! We eventually got back to Tengah to find that all of the leading edges and a lot of the top surface had been stripped back to bare metal by the hail.

'The control column had an explosive charge designed to "snatch" it forward [and disconnect it] should the crew eject. This was to stop the pilot losing his legs! One aircraft had been serviced in Hong Kong, and a little later Dick Shuster was on the approach to Darwin, in northern Australia, when the snatch unit fired [metallic fillings were later found in the electrics], leaving Dick with no elevator control. Darwin is known for the large rise and fall in its runway. Just using the elevator trim, Dick safely landed the aircraft. A few weeks later he completely screwed up a landing at Tengah and the aircraft left the runway with a lot of damage. Subsequently, Dick had an interview with the Station Commander, where he was told that he was to receive the AFC for the first landing and a "bollocking" for the second one!'

AS.30 IN THE FEAF

No 45 Sqn received its first AS.30-capable B 15 (WH977) in June 1966, together with a ground simulator, but the squadron still had only three Canberras (WH961, WH977 and WT213) configured for missile carriage by the end of the year. Thereafter, four Exercise *Hotshots* were mounted, two from Labuan and two from Woomera, during which 128 missiles were fired.

How many personnel does it take to run a Canberra squadron? No 81 Sqn in 1960 at Tengah (*Author*)

A French-built Nord AS.30 air-to-surface missile is loaded onto Canberra B 15 WH961 at Labuan. The post-Confrontation 'flying camel badge' is visible on the aircraft's fin (*via Jefford*)

The farewell formation that marked the disbandment of No 81 Sqn at Tengah on 16 January 1970. According to squadron pilot Alan Harrison, 'The ceremony was timed to end at sunset and the flypast to coincide so that we flew out of the setting sun and into the night. As you would expect of 81, the formation was immaculate – as was the timing' (*Alan Harrison*)

The AS.30 was normally fired at about three-and-a-half miles from its target, rapidly accelerating to near supersonic speed. The target had to be distinct enough to be visible at the time of launch, and the aeroplane had to be high enough to permit it to be seen. The usual technique involved a low-level approach, followed by a pop up to about 1000 ft for launch and a gradual descent during the guidance phase. A significant drawback with this first generation missile was that the launch aircraft had to follow the weapon until its impact, which involved flying very close to the (presumably defended) target.

Simon Baldwin was a navigator on No 45 Sqn from 1964 to 1967;

'During Confrontation there were worries about small ships coming across the short stretches of water that lay between Malaysia and Indonesia, and the wire-guided AS.30 was a more accurate way of responding than a 1000-lb bomb. We would run in at 58 ft to hammer China Rock with gun fire as part of our anti-shipping role. Over land, virtually all of Malaysia was a low-flying area, but the maps were largely featureless. Blue Silk kept unlocking so we tended to navigate by Dead Reckoning and visual lookout. Low-level night attacks were a non-starter because all of our weapon delivery was done visually.'

As the four strike squadrons of Akrotiri's Canberra Wing had disbanded by 17 March 1969, a few of the Near East Air Force's redundant AS.30 carriers were flown out to Tengah. The arrival of WH966 and WH968 in March 1969 allowed No 45 Sqn to dispose of WJ766, its last non-AS.30 aircraft. Several more of Akrotiri's second-hand aeroplanes (and a few 'used' navigators) found their way out to the FEAF simply to sustain No 45 Sqn's strength. After years of punishing low-level flying in the turbulent tropical air, cracks were appearing in the Canberra's wing centre section forging. WT213 was the first to display these symptoms, and it was grounded in March 1969. WH959 and WH961 were similarly diagnosed in May, and two more ex-NEAF missile-firers were ferried out to Singapore as replacements in June. One of the pilots involved was Chris Yeo who would take the UK-prototype of the Eurofighter 2000 on its first flight in April 1994.

As it began to run down, No 45 Sqn mounted a series of five FAC training detachments to Kai Tak while No 81 Sqn continued to operate from there on oblique PR runs looking into China. With the British withdrawal from Singapore, No 81 Sqn disbanded on 16 January 1970, and on 18 February No 45 Sqn followed suit. The latter unit had managed to write off nine Canberras in 14 years, which in Jeff Jefford's words 'was about par for the course back then'.

RAF GERMANY

On 1 January 1958 No 88 Sqn's Wildenrath-based Canberra B(I) 8s and their two-man crews were formally committed to the nuclear strike role. In C-in-C 2nd TAF's words, 'their role is that of night interdictor, but they are also capable of high and "pylon" [low-level] bombing. Much of No 88 Sqn's practice work is now carried out over Denmark. High-level attacks are made to test the air defences, followed by low-level ones on airfields to practise the LABS technique. No 88 Sqn and the other Canberra B(I) 8 units occupy an important place in the 2nd TAF, and the morale of their crews is high. They have absolute trust in their aircraft and are confident of their ability to reach a target anywhere, however small it may be and however limited the visibility. In fact, No 88 Sqn has claimed successful low-level practice attacks with only 450 yards visibility'.

Dick Kidney joined No 88 Sqn as a first tour B(I) 8 pilot, with Martin Watts as his navigator, in July 1959;

'Our primary role then was night ground attack. We operated as pairs using slow flares. The first B(I) 8 would drop its flares while the other attacked the illuminated target, whereupon we would swap positions. The forward-firing 20 mm Hispano guns were awesome – the ammunition weighed a ton before the gun pod went on. We also did day ground attack. We were to aim for the wooded areas of East Germany, looking for Scud [surface-to-surface] missiles rising to the vertical so we could hammer them with cannon fire.

'We had one B(I) 8 armed at all times, with barbed wire around the blast wall, in the southeast corner of Wildenrath. The QRA [quick reaction alert] crew lived in the hangar together with the US Alert Duty Officer. It was an 80- to 100-yard sprint to the aircraft, so three service bicycles, each painted red, were positioned in the hangar – one for the pilot, one for the nav and one for the Yank.'

No 102 Sqn had morphed into No 59 Sqn in August 1956, and the latter unit operated the B 2 until April 1957, when it started converting to the B(I) 8. Having moved to Geilenkirchen on 15 November 1957, No 59 Sqn deployed to Akrotiri with No 88 Sqn in July 1958 when Operation *Dimension* was mounted after it was feared that anarchy in the Lebanon would lead to a coup in Jordan. No 59 Sqn would return to Geilenkirchen in mid-August, remaining there until 4 January 1961 when it re-numbered as No 3 Sqn.

Canberra upgrading, combined with cutbacks generated by

Mean machine – a No 14 Sqn Canberra B(I) 8 with its trademark offset canopy at Wildenrath in 1966 (*National Aerospace Library*)

Duncan Sandys' 1957 Defence White Paper, resulted in the following Canberra B(I) 6 and B(I) 8 squadron number plates in RAF Germany;

Squadron	Base	Aircraft	Dates
No 3 Sqn	RAF Geilenkirchen	B(I) 8	1/61 to 1/68
No 3 Sqn	RAF Laarbruch	B(I) 8	1/68 to 1/72
No 14 Sqn	RAF Wildenrath	B(I) 8	12/62 to 1/70
No 16 Sqn	RAF Laarbruch	B(I) 8	3/58 to 6/72
No 59 Sqn*	RAF Geilenkirchen	B(I) 8	11/57 to 1/61
No 88 Sqn**	RAF Wildenrath	B(I) 8	1/56 to 12/62
No 213 Sqn	RAF Bruggen	B(I) 6	8/57 to 12/69

*Renumbered No 3 Sqn
**Renumbered No 14 Sqn

A single Canberra from each of the four squadrons was on QRA initially. Ray Leach, a first tour navigator with No 16 Sqn, was on QRA at the height of the Cuban crisis in 1962 when the commitment was doubled up to two aircraft per squadron, and it stayed that way. They had to be airborne within 15 minutes of an alert, these Canberras providing an immediate response to SACEUR's call for single strikes, or as the vanguard of a fully generated force.

With the assumption of the nuclear role, No 88 Sqn should have relinquished its previously assigned roles of army cooperation and close air support, but life was never that simple. In Dick Kidney's words, 'we kept our ground attack skills for deployments. For instance, in June 1961 I was woken at 5 am as Iraq was threatening Kuwait. We loaded up with 1000-lb bombs and guns and set off for Akrotiri – the first half-dozen or so crews to arrive in Cyprus had a quick rest and then flew in a straight line to Sharjah with no flight plan, no nav lights and no radio transmissions.

'The targets we were given included Iraqi radar sites and the Ministry of Defence building in Baghdad. I was expected to strafe the fourth and fifth floors with cannon – I was told to avoid the lower floors, which accommodated Western female typists. People had great faith in our pinpoint capability.

'Most of our subsequent flying over Germany was without the gun pod fitted. It was a bit of a fag to install and remove the gun pack, but we kept current over the Nordhorn range and the Strohen range west of Brunswick.'

Phil Wilkinson joined No 14 Sqn at Wildenrath with his navigator, Paddy O'Shea, in November 1963, by which time the nuclear strike role was well established. In Phil's words, 'the next three years' routine featured repetitive training in the attack profile, involving long-range low-level sorties [250 ft AGL in peacetime], visiting at least one weapon range per sortie, culminating in a LABS manoeuvre to throw a 25-lb practice bomb at the target.

'The attack was a trifle mechanical, and involved pre-computing release parameters prior to take-off, which were then fed into the release computer at the rear of the aircraft by the navigator before the crew clambered on board. For both the standard forward toss and reversionary "over the shoulder" attacks, the approach speed was calculated from met data to give an Equivalent Air Speed of 434 knots. The pull-up was triggered by

Pilot Phil Wilkinson (left) and his navigator Paddy O'Shea, both of No 14 Sqn, at El Adem, Libya, on 28 February 1966 (*Phil Wilkinson*)

pressing the bomb release button at the final IP [Initial Point] and waiting until the computer-driven timer ran down and gave the cue. The pilot had a LABS instrument that helped him maintain accuracy in roll and pitch. Basically, he had to keep two needles at right angles to each other between guidelines across the face of the instrument. The Canberra was a responsive aircraft, but at the normal attack speed of nearly 450 knots, the pull-up of around +3.4g was a bit of a challenge.

'This was an arcade game for real, and the bomb would be launched during this looping manoeuvre – usually at around 60-70 degrees on the way up the climb – and be thrown well forward as the Canberra recovered from the top of the loop, rolled to wings level and descended rapidly to low-level again. This mildly aerobatic escape recovery from 4000+ ft back down to 250 ft offered some protection from the blast effect of the exploding weapon.'

Range work on Nordhorn and other northern European ranges, and also at Tarhuna, in Libya, was crucial for consistent proficiency and accuracy, interspersed with NATO exercises. *Blue Moon* and *Cold Fire* were ATAF-wide events, while *Highwood* and *Priory* saw RAF Germany units exercising with the UK Air Defence Region. Finally, someone with a sense of humour came up with *Cloggy Emotion* to exercise Dutch FACs.

The B(I) 8 Interdiction role now focused on striking at Warsaw Pact airfields hosting attack assets. In an effort to also remain semi-prepared for short notice contingencies, all Canberra squadrons had at least one three-week detachment to Cyprus in the conventional fit. Known as Exercise *Citrus Grove*, crews dive-bombed raft targets in Episkopi Bay and strafed targets on the Larnaca salt flats. There was hardly a day when a singleton aircraft and crew was not somewhere down the Southern or Extended Southern Ranger route through the Gulf and on to Aden, Nairobi and Salisbury. Return routes often staged via Tehran, and then had extended low-level sectors across Iran before climbing out to overfly Turkey and returning to Germany via Cyprus, or after some Libyan desert low-flying.

In mid-1966 the Mk 7 1650-lb bomb that required a LABS manoeuvre for accurate delivery was replaced by the US Mk 43 2100-lb weapon,

Brüggen-based Canberra B(I) 6 WT316 of No 213 was photographed during a refuelling stop somewhere in France in the 1960s. Its low-level camouflage scheme is 'a variegated pattern of greys and greens', while the tail motif is a hornet – long synonymous with the squadron (*Peter Green Collection*)

Eric Tilsley tucks the gear up but keeps the nose down in his No 213 Sqn Canberra B(I) 6 as he takes off from Brüggen in early 1969 – the unit disbanded in December of that same year. Single stores pylons, capable of carrying a 1000-lb bomb apiece, are clearly visible under each wing. (*Peter Green Collection*)

which could be dropped from a high-speed, lay-down attack courtesy of parachute retardation. According to Phil Wilkinson, 'I don't think we were ever told what the time delay was to be before detonation, which strikes me today as a little worrying. No 14 Sqn resumed QRA with the new weapon on 4 November 1966. We began to get quite clever with the SFOM sight fitted in the bomb-aimer's position, and even more so with the essential Chinagraph marks placed on the widescreen. LABS scores were customarily achieved in the order of 100 or so yards – lay-down could reduce that to just tens of feet'.

The navigation fit consisted of a first generation Doppler known as Blue Silk, which was the precursor of Green Satin. It was then decided to add the Decca Mk 8, and Ray Leach flew on the trials. 'We added an extra navigator and flew hi-lo-hi to and from Germany to attack Henstridge airfield in Somerset. One nav map-read down the nose while the other plotted on the desk. The trial proved the Decca to be ideal for "flying a trawler", but it was fitted anyway. I spent most of my time navigating the B(I) 8 by map-reading down the nose. I flew Laarbruch-Bahrain-Sharjah-Aden and back via El Adem and Malta using Dead Reckoning, a pair of binoculars and a set of topos. On interdiction sorties, the nav turned the pilot towards the target and left him to fire the gun.'

Phil Wilkinson proclaimed that 'the abilities of the navigator fraternity were remarkable. Their working environment in the B(I)8 was testing to say the least – 90 per cent of the time stretched out in the nose map-reading, contorting back at regular intervals to update the navigation equipment from the most recent visual fix'.

There was no ejection seat for the B(I) 8 navigator. In an emergency he had to jettison the crew door and roll out of the doomed Canberra. That was the default position on Valiant, Victor and Vulcan bombers too, and as on the V-force, when a Canberra 'went in' at low-level it usually claimed the lives of all on board. Of the 57 B(I) 8s that were built, 51 were divided up between three RAF Germany squadrons. Of these, 12 were lost and 15 aircrew died. Even worse was the loss rate of the B(I) 6s, which were flown exclusively by No 213 Sqn. Of the 19 taken on strength, eight were lost. The B(I) 6 carried a crew of three – all with ejection seats – and 20 were killed in flying accidents.

IMPROVED PHOTO-RECCE

By the mid-1950s the PR Meteor was no match for Warsaw Pact fighters, and the arrival of the Swift FR 5, Hunter FR 10 and PR Canberra gave RAF Germany a much improved reconnaissance capability. Four PR Canberra squadrons were established on the 'Clutch' airfields beginning with No 69 Sqn, which had re-formed with PR 3s at Laarbruch by the end of 1954. It was followed by No 31 Sqn, which re-formed at Laarbruch on 1 March 1955 with PR 7s. On 15 June 1955, No 214 Sqn re-formed at RAF Laarbruch, but on 1 August that same year it was renumbered No 80 Sqn to operate PR 7s. The fourth PR Canberra unit to join the 2nd TAF was No 17 Sqn, which re-formed at Wahn on 1 June 1956. In April 1957 No 17 Sqn moved to Wildenrath and in June No 80 Sqn went to Brüggen. No 69 Sqn moved to Luqa on 1 April 1958, where it was renumbered No 39 Sqn shortly thereafter.

The No 31 Sqn ORB recorded that in January 1957 its Canberra PR 7s were being equipped with Green Satin, and its associated GPI (Ground Position Indicator), which, in Tony Burt's words, 'were a boon to navigators. The equipment gave the navigator a constant readout of his ground position – provided always that the Doppler radar locked on and supplied continuous drift and groundspeed which, computed with True Air Speed and true computer heading, translated into ground position. Generally interpreted as latitude and longitude, it could also be read as "along and across track". The equipment first appeared in my logbook when, on 14 November 1958, with "Red" Dunningham in WT514, I logged "Base. BZ low flying area Green Satin Test".

'The longest PR 7 sortie that I logged with No 31 Sqn was with Wg Cdr Kennedy in WT511 on 16 October 1958. We were airborne that day at 1340 hrs for a sortie of 5 hrs 10 min on Exercise *Sunbeam* on Raid 55/10. We flew again the following day on Raid 137/5 of *Sunbeam* – and again on the 18th for Raid 186/7 of the same exercise – but I logged no details of the route! It sounds as though we were flying as "raiders" against defence systems. I only flew one longer sortie in a Canberra PR 7 – which came on 20 November 1968. This was a transit flight of 5 hrs 15 min from Nicosia to Masirah in WH801 with Flt Lt Reeves while on No 17 Sqn based at Wildenrath (my second PR 7 tour).

'One shorter French cross-country flight highlighted an aspect of our high altitude sorties. On 28 November 1957 I flew with Flt Lt Edwards in WJ816 on the route Grenoble-Corsica-Bordeaux and back to base in a time of 3 hrs 35 min. We cruise climbed to 48,000 ft, and our photography was done over southern France. It was routine for us to fly above the airways traffic as "Military Air Traffic", and to make full use of our ability to climb to height. It was on one of these high-level reconnaissance cross-countries over France that I experienced the "bends" for the one and only time as we flew north to base! My knee hurt appreciably but we were able to route so as to descend gradually, and I suffered no after effects!'

Alan Harrison was another navigator on No 31 Sqn;

'The PR 7 was lengthened between the cockpit and wing to accommodate the forward camera bay. Also, half of the bomb-bay was converted into a fuel tank while the other half was designed to carry 256 flares. With wingtip tanks, the aircraft carried 27,000 lbs of fuel in an

No 31 Sqn Canberra PR 7 WH775 returns to its Mobile Field Photographic Unit at Laarbruch during a rapid film display for NATO VIPs in September 1964
(*Graham Pitchfork*)

airframe that weighed 25,000 lbs when empty. We had a range of more than 3000 nautical miles and could reach heights in excess of 50,000 ft.'

The PR 7 could range anywhere along the NATO front from Norway to the Mediterranean.

Graham Pitchfork was one of the first navigators to go through Cranwell, and although he was 'invited' to volunteer for the shiny new V-Force, he was posted instead to No 101(PR) Course at RAF Bassingbourn in September 1961. 'On arrival I met my pilot, Terry Close, who had just "escaped" from the V-Force after a tour as a co-pilot. We learned that we had been posted to No 81 Sqn in Singapore, but with just two weeks to go, No 31 Sqn lost a crew in a tragic flying accident. NATO was deemed to have a higher priority than the Far East, and Terry and I found ourselves cancelling our tropical kit and heading for Laarbruch to join the "Goldstars" in April 1962.

'A few days after joining No 31 Sqn, I was programmed to fly a check ride with the CO, Charles Dalziel. There were five targets in the British Zone, culminating with a "military installation" close to a canal south of Bremen. All went well until this final target. We set off from the IP and at the appointed time there was nothing that looked remotely like a military target. I was to learn later that this was the CO's party piece for all new navigators.

'When the film arrived, the CO took me through it until the fifth target ought to have appeared. He had taken some photographs and I could just about make out some old and derelict buildings. I enquired if that was the target? "Yes, my boy," came the reply, "there are the remains of the camp where Herr Hitler incarcerated me for some time after I had been shot down". He then gave me the most important piece of advice for those in the PR business. "Always take a photograph at the elapsed time, as the photo interpreter may find what he is looking for even if you don't see it". And with that he took me off to the bar.'

Graham was later to discover 'the need for the navigator to operate the cameras from the nose and the photo-flash controls from his seat in the rear of the cockpit. For difficult targets this led to the need for two navigators, although crews were established for one only. Flying at 1200 ft and emitting a few million candle power every two seconds made one feel somewhat vulnerable.

'At an early stage in the transition to war, the PR squadrons would disperse four or five aircraft to bare bases, taking an element of their mobile field photographic unit with them. Conditions at airstrips such as De Peel, in Holland, were very basic. We had no specific war role. When the hooter went, the recce squadrons would immediately launch two aircraft to cover likely enemy lines of advance. As we taxied back in, the groundcrew whipped off the camera magazines, which would be rushed away. We debriefed, and within 20 minutes the photos would appear.

'Following increased tension after the erection of the Berlin Wall, a number of Inner German border recce flights were flown using an oblique mounted F52 camera with a 48-in lens. I recall using the airfield at Celle, where a flight of No 5 Sqn Javelins provided us with a fighter escort during our photo runs up and down the border.'

Nos 17, 31 and 80 Sqns were predominantly low-level pre- and post-strike reconnaissance squadrons, with the emphasis being placed on daylight missions. However, Dick Kidney, who flew PR 7s with both Nos 80 and No 31 Sqns, recalls pushing out 18 photo-flashes in quick succession to secure wide-area night photo coverage.

From a groundcrew perspective, the Canberra was a very straightforward 'tube with wings', and in the words of Terry O'Halloran, an airframe fitter on No 31 Sqn from 1965-68, 'we enjoyed working on it. We had to fit or remove the tip tanks depending on the task, and that was a job!'

Competitions were a major feature of the NATO reconnaissance scene in the 1960s. *Day* and *Night Royal Flush* were just two names that evoke mixed emotions among ex-reconnaissance personnel. There was doubtless some value in these competitions, particularly for the photographers and photo interpreters, but the majority of squadron crews were not involved. In Graham Pitchfork's opinion, 'TACEVALs and exercises involving the whole squadron provided a great deal more realistic training that led to operational benefits and efficiency'. But whatever the training regime, by the end of the 1960s the increasing capability of Warsaw Pact air defences demanded more sophisticated

Canberra B(I) 8 XM278 of No 14 Sqn being flown by Phil Wilkinson over Germany on 10 June 1966. It was photographed by Dickie Lees from a Canberra PR 7 of No 17 Sqn. Following its retirement from RAF service in 1972, XM278 was sold to Marshall's of Cambridge and converted into a B(I) 68 for the Peruvian Air Force (*Phil Wilkinson*)

sensors and better aircraft performance than the PR 7 could provide. Consequently, No 80 Sqn disbanded at Brüggen on 30 September 1969, No 17 Sqn disbanded at Wildenrath on 31 December and No 31 Sqn disbanded at Laarbruch on 31 March 1971.

The first of the 2nd TAF's Canberra strike/interdictor squadrons to disband was No 213 Sqn on 31 December 1969. No 14 Sqn converted to the Phantom FGR 2 at the end of June 1970 and No 3 Sqn converted to the Harrier GR 1 at the end of 1971. In June 1972 No 16 Sqn began converting to the Buccaneer S 2. The retirement of No 16 Sqn's B(I) 8s marked the end of the 21-year strike career of the RAF's first jet bomber.

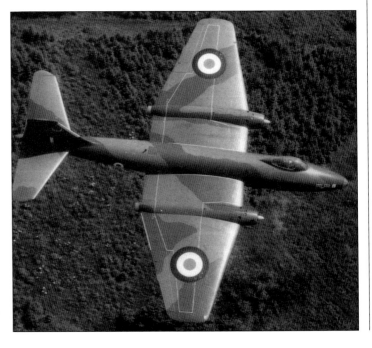

ULTIMATE PR 9

The Special Radio Installation Flight of No 192 Sqn at Watton, in Norfolk, received two Canberra B 2s in February 1953. They were joined by two B 6s in December 1954, and all four jets were refitted for Radio Proving Flights (RPF) – a euphemism for secret Signal Intelligence (Sigint) operations along the rim of the Warsaw Pact, interspersed with longer trips around the Baltic and the Mediterranean. These Canberras would act as 'ferrets' in concert with No 192 Sqn's specially modified Washington B 1s, flying high and fast to trigger the opposing air defences and communications, or sometimes 'popping up' from low level. Up to ten Special Operators were carried in the Washingtons to record and analyse the responses, but there was only one 'Spec Op' in the Canberra sitting next to the navigator.

The first missions flown by No 192 Sqn Canberras were probably part of Operation *Reason*, a series of flights over the Baltic, Black and Caspian Seas during 1953-54. The flights were staged out of Bodö, Wunstorf, Luqa and Nicosia, and in May 1954 the first signals from a Soviet air intercept radar – the 'Scan Odd' fitted in the MiG-17 – were collected over the Caspian. Each RPF had to be approved by the Prime Minister, and the main justification was to sustain the close and profitable air intelligence relationship with the US. As CAS briefed the PM in June 1955, 'this can only continue if we are able to put valuable information into the common pool'.

RPFs also brought back data that was key to the design of the electronic warning and countermeasures equipment fitted in the V-bombers. In October 1956 valuable intelligence on the Yak-25 interceptor was gained during a Washington/Canberra mission over the Barents Sea. A new Soviet height-finding radar was identified and VHF (as distinct from HF) communications between Soviet air defence ground stations were recorded for the first time.

The Washingtons were replaced by Comet C 2Rs after 1957, and No 192 Sqn became No 51 Sqn in August 1958. By then it was operating three Canberra B 6s and two B 2s, and over the following two years the B 6s received new British-designed Sigint sensors – the AR 18050/18058 (Breton) high-band system for Electronic Intelligence and low-band systems such as the ARI 18176 (Overcoat) VHF receiver. What became known as B 6(RC)s were fitted with an extended rounded nose radome and new tape recorders, but despite the technological advances, the missions remained much the same – probing Warsaw Pact air defences and listening to transmissions on behalf of GCHQ.

During Operation *Duster* during the Middle East crisis of 1973, Sigint Nimrods flew along the Egyptian and Syrian coasts while Canberra

Flt Lt David Robinson and Sqn Ldr John Harrington with their 'special' Canberra B 2 at Wyton in 1957 (*Peter Green Collection*)

B 6(RC)s operated out of Luqa along the Libyan coast. No 51 Sqn, which moved to Wyton in 1963, lost its Canberras in October 1976, partly on cost grounds but also because up-close-and-personal RPFs were facing more frequent airborne interceptions.

Canberra B 6(BS) WJ768 of No 51 Sqn at Gütersloh in October 1973. The distinctive Blue Shadow aerial can be clearly seen on the side of the forward fuselage. This aircraft had previously seen combat with No 139 Sqn during the Suez campaign of 1956 (*SG-ETUO/Erich Westersötebier*)

PHOTO SPECIALS

On 1 March 1954, Canberra PR 3 WH726 was flown to the US by a No 58 Sqn crew. It was to be modified at Hanscom AFB, near Boston, to accept a 240-in focal length framing camera that had been specially designed for Long-Range Oblique Photography (LOROP). Known colloquially as 'The Bomb Camera', it must have been designed specifically for the B-57/Canberra because it fitted neatly into the bomb-bay using the existing lugs. After WH726 returned to the UK, it was used by No 58 Sqn to take pictures through a large optical window cut in the aircraft's port lower fuselage. With a second Canberra flying alongside to warn of contrails, WH726 flew at least nine LOROP missions over Central Europe and the eastern Mediterranean, returning with useful imagery of 'denied territory' taken from high inside friendly airspace. Use of this formidable piece of folding optics was known as Operation *Robin*.

On 29 August 1955, a Canberra B 2 test bed fitted with a pair of Olympus engines reached 65,889 ft, which leads us neatly to the 'Top Gear' sports version of the Canberra, the PR 9. The latter was conceived as the RAF's answer to the U-2, the prototype first flying on 27 July 1958. With powered flying controls, an autopilot, bigger wings and much more powerful Avon 206 engines (rated at 11,250 lbs of thrust each), the PR 9 was designed to operate at altitudes in excess of 60,000 ft. It had a redesigned nose similar to the B(I) 8, but with an opening canopy that was a boon in hot climates. Access to the navigator's forward station was through a sideways-opening nose, and he had an ejection seat from the second production aircraft onwards.

Production of 23 PR 9s was subcontracted to Shorts of Belfast, and 21 aircraft were delivered to the RAF. In 1959 a flight of Canberra PR 9s was established within PR 7-equipped No 58 Sqn at Wyton, from where trained crews and aircraft moved out to No 13 Sqn in Cyprus in 1961 and No 39 Sqn in Malta in 1962. The high-flying PR 9s remained with No 58 Sqn for two years, despite the unit being earmarked for use in war by SACEUR as Bomber Command's key low-level tactical reconnaissance asset. Indeed, during 1955 No 58 Sqn's PR 7s had surveyed part of Kenya in support of anti-Mau Mau operations, and the unit continued to undertake low-level reconnaissance with PR 7s until it disbanded in 1970.

Canberra PR 9 XH173 of No 39 Sqn in the mid-1960s. Delivered to the RAF in September 1960, this aircraft initially served with No 58 Sqn before alternating between Nos 13 and 39 Sqns. Ending up with No 1 PRU, XH173 was passed on to the Chilean Air Force in October 1982 (*Peter Green Collection*)

Vernon Harding completed three squadron tours as a navigator on the PR 9;

'In the early days, the aircraft was easily able to sustain level flight at just over 60,000 ft, but later on, probably because of increases in its weight and dents and twists in the airframe, 58,000 ft became a more realistic figure.

'Flying at high altitudes meant that image degradation was greater due to the effects of the atmosphere. To overcome these problems, the PR 9 was equipped with a much developed and improved suite of cameras. The F49 Mk 4 survey camera was gyro-stabilised and mounted in a nitrogen-filled pod. It marked the first occasion that a camera was pod-mounted on the PR Canberra – a system which was to prove very successful with later sensor fits.

'For high-level reconnaissance, the PR 9 had a number of F96 cameras mounted either in a fan of two or four, providing a wide-angle of cover, or, in the oblique mode, set across the aircraft at angles of 15 or 18 degrees below the horizontal. These F96 cameras were fitted with lenses of either 24- or 48-in focal length, and they had an image movement compensation system that improved resolution. For low-level operations, the PR 9 had three of the same F95 cameras that were fitted to the PR 7. It also had a night low-level camera.'

The PR 9 entered RAF service at around the time Gary Powers was shot down in his U-2 on 1 May 1960. Chris Pocock is clear that 'the U-2 offered performance that those who designed and flew Canberras could only dream of', so some changes had to be made to the employment plans of the PR 9.

Both Nos 13 and 39 Sqns flew the PR 9 in the Mediterranean, the latter unit being based at Luqa and No 13 Sqn flip-flopping between Cyprus and Malta as political imperatives changed. No 39 Sqn operated mainly to the north and west of Malta while No 13 Sqn focused its activities to the south and east. Apart from aerial survey work, No 39 Sqn was assigned

Canberra PR 7 WT537 of No 13 Sqn at Wyton on 21 August 1971. Delivered to the RAF in December 1955, this aircraft served with Nos 17 and 31 Sqns before completing it service career with No 13 Sqn. Sold off to BAE in November 1981, it was the gate guard at Samlesbury until 2009, when it was removed for possible restoration (*Peter Green Collection*)

to NATO's southern region in the low-level role, spending much flying time over Italy and Greece. Nonetheless, there was a constant demand for high-level national reconnaissance tasking from the Near East out to the Far East. Almost permanent No 13 Sqn detachments were maintained in Bahrain and Aden, while crews were sent to Singapore to support No 81 Sqn during Confrontation. In Vernon Harding's words, 'there was also a fair amount of tasking in North Africa and the occasional trip to Hong Kong. Make no mistake, the living was good!'

No 39 Sqn was rather more static, being based at Wyton from 1 October 1970 and assigned to support NATO's Northern Flank in the low-level reconnaissance role. Its forward operating base was at Ørland, near the mouth of the Trondheim fjord – Dick Kidney recalled climbing out of Norwegian fjords much more powerfully in a PR 9 than in a PR 7. A number of three- and four-ship detachments were sent to the Far East, whilst survey tasking was also undertaken in the New Hebrides, Fiji, Jamaica and in Africa.

No 13 Sqn joined No 39 Sqn at Wyton on 22 October 1978, by which time the former was operating a mixed fleet of PR 7s and PR 9s. This arrangement allowed some PR 9s to be put into storage to preserve their fatigue life, and by the time No 13 Sqn disbanded in January 1982, it was operating PR 7s only. Assigned to Allied Forces Southern Europe, the unit spent a lot of time at its Forward Operating Base of Villafranca, near Verona.

No 39 Sqn was now the only unit flying the PR 9, and when it too disbanded on 1 June 1982, five of the squadron's aircraft were used to reform No 1 Photographic Reconnaissance Unit (PRU).

Simon Baldwin served as Station Commander at Wyton from 1985 to 1987. He recalled that the varied tasks flown by PR 9 crews at high altitude and low-level provided good training for whatever tasks they might have to fly in war. In addition to the cameras, the ex-Phantom II Infra-Red Line Scan (IRLS) was fitted in the former F49 camera pod, and it could be used at low level, although crews frequently flew along the East German border at high altitude.

Wyton-based Canberra PR 9s XH133 and XH168 of No 39 Sqn fly over Norway during a detachment in the early 1970s. The unit became a familiar sight in Scandinavian skies during this period as it was charged with supporting NATO's Northern Flank in the low-level reconnaissance role. No 39 Sqn's forward operating base was at Ørland, near the mouth of the Trondheim fjord (National Aerospace Library)

'Hemp' was the colour scheme adopted by RAF tankers and surveillance aircraft in the late 1980s, with the handful of Canberra PR 9s in frontline service with Strike Command being repainted accordingly. No 39 Sqn's XH134 was amongst those jets, the aircraft being put through its paces in this 1993 photograph. No 1 PRU had become No 39 Sqn (1 PRU) the previous year (MoD)

No 39 Sqn Canberra PR 9 XH169 taxies out at Entebbe airport, in Uganda, at the start of a mission over neighbouring Rwanda in December 1996. The aircraft was detached to the region for four weeks as part of an RAF photo-reconnaissance party charged with monitoring the Rwandan refugee crisis. The RAF component of the party comprised some 40 personnel from No 39 Sqn, including engineers, a fully equipped photo processing and interpretation unit, a small RAF Police unit and a medic from the Tactical Medical Wing at RAF Lyneham. The team was flown to Entebbe by a No 10 Sqn VC10 and the detachment was supported by regular Hercules flights from RAF Lyneham (*HQ STC*)

No 1 PRU later moved to Marham, and low-level flying virtually ceased so as to extend PR 9 fatigue life. The weakest point of the airframe was the pressure bulkhead at the back of the cockpit, and as one of the PRU's PR 9s reached the end of its fatigue life, it was replaced by another taken out of storage. The unit was renamed No 39 (1 PRU) Sqn on 1 July 1992. While extensive surveys were flown over Zimbabwe and Kenya, national tasking steadily increased and operations were flown over the former republic of Yugoslavia on behalf of the UN and NATO. Sorties were also performed over Afghanistan, Bosnia, Iraq and Somalia.

Despite its advancing years, the PR 9 still climbed faster than anything else in the RAF until Typhoon arrived.

In the mid-1990s, the Canberra Sensor System Upgrade added new panoramic and mapping cameras, and a long-range sideways-looking electro-optical sensor (EOS) that could be data-linked to a ground station. The PR 9 navigator sat ahead of the pilot in the enclosed nose, where two very small windows on either side at head level were jokingly described as 'day-night indicators'. The navigator controlled three of the four sensor systems, the exception being the F95 low-level cameras with 4- or 12-in lenses and 70 mm film, three of which looked left, right and ahead from their fixed positions in the nose. The pilot controlled these reminders that the PR 9 could perform the 'tactical' as well as the 'strategic' reconnaissance role. But they were only used occasionally towards the end.

To his left, the navigator had a control panel for the Zeiss RMK – a survey camera that replaced the old F49. The Zeiss RMK viewed the ground vertically through a circular window in the rear fuselage. No 39 (1 PRU) Sqn deployed six times to Kenya and Zimbabwe between 1996 and 2001 for photo-mapping, although the Zeiss camera was also used over Afghanistan, Iraq, Rwanda and Somalia for military purposes. The navigator had a 'recce sight' – a periscope with fore-and-aft steering – that presented the ground beneath to him through a nosecone in the middle of the front panel. Correcting for velocity and height, he called out small course corrections to the pilot above and behind him.

Simon Baldwin regards the Canberra PR 9 as 'the only aircraft I have flown that was built around the navigator, with everything (apart from the IFF selector) in the right places'.

Between 1978 and 1980, 12 of the surviving 16 PR 9s were given a better Doppler, along with a Decca Tactical Air Navigation System to improve track keeping. An updated Radar Warning System was simultaneously mounted on the tail. Much later, a very accurate embedded GPS/INS was added. This was essential if the new EOS, with its very long focal length, was to be accurately pointed at its pre-planned targets. In RAF service, the EOS was known as the Rapid Deployment Electro-Optical System (RADEOS). Manufactured by Goodrich in the US, it was also utilised by USAF U-2s. For the

Canberra, a new gimbal and crate assembly was built so that the sensor could be carried in the PR 9's former photo-flare bay. This bay once housed either the IRLS or System III, a 36-in focal length camera with seven 'stop-and-shoot' positions that was also derived from the U-2. By Gulf War II in March 2003 both of these sensors had been retired.

The 'fantastic' EOS in the flare bay weighed 1500 lbs and measured 8 ft by 3 ft. EOS imagery was datalinked to a ground station and was inter-operable with US systems. When the PR 9 flew beyond the ground station's line-of-sight (as over Afghanistan), the imagery was recorded onboard for later relay, or replay on the ground. RADEOS could photograph the Houses of Parliament from 47,000 ft over the Isle of Wight, and the time on 'Big Ben' would be clearly visible.

The EOS brought the Canberra into the modern world of 'real-time' reconnaissance, and the EO sensor cut through haze to produce very high-quality daytime imagery at very long standoff range. However, its field-of-view was very narrow, which made the fourth item in the PR 9's sensor suite so useful. The KA-93 panoramic camera, made by Recon/Optical, provided wide-angle coverage from the horizon to the vertical on both sides of the flightpath using a 24-in focal length lens. It occupied the Canberra's forward camera bay, beneath which were small sliding doors that opened in flight so that the camera's scanning element (a rotating prism) could be lowered into position. A huge amount of territory could be captured on the KA-93's five-inch roll film at high resolution, with stereo overlap.

The overall PR 9 system was both successful and popular, and in its final years many UK and US commanders would put 'Preferred Sensor Canberra PR 9' on their reconnaissance request forms.

Fourteen aircrew and 105 groundcrew kept the PRU's five PR 9s and two T 4 trainers flying. In support were 14 imagery analysts, 25 wet film photo engineers/developers and four people from the Air Survey Liaison Section who made up maps. They all combined to achieve a 95 per cent serviceability

Film canisters are removed from XH169 at Entebbe in December 1996, the jet having completed yet another Rwanda flight. BOZ-107 chaff/flare dispenser pods can been seen on each of the underwing stores pylons (*HQ STC*)

Nose art was applied to two of the three No 39 Sqn Canberra PR 9s that flew in Operation *Telic* in 2003. XH168 was *Eastern Promise* while XH169 was *Persian Princess*. Both aircraft also carried Scud-hunt mission marks – the red crosses superimposed on each indicated that this was a fruitless search (*No 39 Sqn Association*)

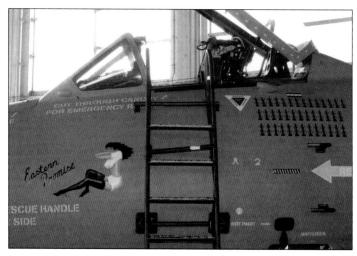

rate during Operation *Telic* in 2003 when two PR 9s were deployed to support the invasion of Iraq.

Why was the PR 9 required over Kosovo, Afghanistan and Iraq? Boasting a range of nearly 2000 nautical miles, the aircraft was unique, as no other reconnaissance platform could carry four different and complementary imaging systems at the same time as high as 50,000 ft for up to five hours.

No 39 Sqn completed 150 missions during the 2003 Iraqi conflict, flying twice daily from its base at Azraq, in Jordan. 'Our initial tasking,' recalled one aircrew member, 'was in the western Iraqi desert, Scud hunting. We flew three missions a day, each nine hours solid, looking at 17 "areas of interest". We data linked most of our imagery and the photo interpreters scanned for Scuds, but none were found'. Such was the quality of the wet film imagery gathered by the unit, a photograph taken from 47,000 ft over Basra showed skid marks from a bus crashed on a bombed bridge.

It was a similar story 12 months earlier when the squadron made an unpublicised excursion – Operation *Ramson* – to Mombasa to look for terrorist threats in Somalia. From an offshore position in international airspace, the PR 9's sensors provided good coverage of Mogadishu and other coastal regions. That deployment took place from March to May 2002 – only two months after the squadron had returned from Operations *Veritas* and *Oracle*. These were Britain's contribution to the defeat of the Taliban regime in Afghanistan, during which No 39 Sqn flew out of Seeb, in Oman, from October 2001 to January 2002.

Terry Cairns flew the PR 9 for much of the time between 1985 and 2006, and he recalls that 'the pressure-breathing kit was in use during my time in Iraq and Afghanistan'. It was said that the PR 9s ranged as far north as Kabul, ending up landing back on fumes on the Seeb taxiway. It was a great tale, although in Terry Cairns' words 'one nutter loitered at altitude over Seeb just to see how long he could stay airborne – and this with the bar open! Our average sortie length was 4 hrs 30 min. We certainly did not use the secondary runway because there wasn't one. The taxiway could be used in an emergency if the main runway was blocked'.

While flying from Basra over southern Iraq between 4 August and 16 September 2003, taking imagery for survey maps of British forces' area of responsibility, the PR 9s produced 6368 prints, together with 239 photo-mosaics and more than 600 maps while looking for illegal border crossings, oil smugglers and escaping terrorists. Panoramic reconnaissance and survey mapping represented 70 per cent of the PR 9s' tasking during

Canberra PR 9 XH135 of No 39 Sqn takes off from Kandahar in 2005 during the unit's penultimate operational deployment with the jet. The veteran aircraft continued to provide valuable high-quality imagery on a daily basis, spending their last deployment (of five months) undertaking sorties over Afghanistan from Seeb, in Oman. Jets were flown into Kandahar mid mission, where the Canberras were refuelled and maintained as necessary. On one sortie over Afghanistan a PR 9 was fired upon by a surface-to-air missile, although with its exceptional rate of climb the aircraft was able to out-manoeuvre the weapon (*RAF Marham*)

Telic. Despite the aircrafts' heavy workload, in early November 2003 two PR 9s departed for the Falkland Islands and a new survey task. No 39 (1 PRU) Sqn was the busiest unit at Marham for two years, and 70 per cent of its output was still wet film.

Simon Baldwin believes that there was such a generation gap in capability between the PR 9 and what went before 'we shouldn't have called it a Canberra. I was air attaché in Washington during Gulf War I, and the PR 9s brought great imagery back, which was shown to Gen Colin Powell. "Why can't we do this?" was his response. "Why do I have to get this from the RAF?"' The PR 9 could take panoramic photographs at the same time as employing its EOS – the U-2 could not do that'.

The final PR 9 flight landed at Kemble on 31 July 2006. The total annual cost of operating No 39 Sqn at the end was very close to £15 million, but money was never going to be found to overcome the pressure bulkhead fatigue issue, and the fact that the ejection seats were becoming increasingly difficult to certify. The last T 4 having been retired on 1 September 2005, the RAF could not keep relying on 'old and bold' PR 9 aircrew either.

A total of 782 Canberras had seen RAF service over 55 years, and the PR 9 had served the nation well, but now it was time to move on.

Canberra PR 9 XH135, along with sister-aircraft XH131, conducted No 39 Sqn's final Afghanistan deployment between January and June 2006. This photograph was taken on 26 June when both aircraft returned to their Marham home from Seeb (*RAF Marham*)

No 39 Sqn's last three Canberra PR 9s, XH131, XH134 and XH135, parked side-by-side on the Marham flightline on 26 June 2006. OC No 39 Sqn, Wg Cdr Clive Mitchell, told the assembled press who were there to witness the jets' return that 'It is time for the Canberra to go. The aircraft has become expensive and difficult to support. It's an economic reality' (*RAF Marham*)

APPENDICES

MAIN CANBERRA SQUADRONS IN ORDER OF FORMATION

SQUADRON	WHERE FORMED	DATE	PREVIOUS AIRCRAFT
No 101	Binbrook	May 1951	Lincoln B 2
No 617	Binbrook	January 1952	Lincoln B 2
No 12	Binbrook	March 1952	Lincoln B 2
No 9	Binbrook	May 1952	Lincoln B 2
No 109	Hemswell	August 1952	Mosquito B 35
No 50	Binbrook	August 1952	Lincoln B 2
No 540(PR)	Benson	December 1952	Mosquito PR 34A
No 10	Scampton	January 1953	Dakota
No 149	Coningsby	March 1953	Washington B 1
No 44	Coningsby	April 1953	Washington B 1
No 57	Honington	May 1953	Washington B 1
No 15	Coningsby	May 1953	Washington B 1
No 27	Scampton	June 1953	Dakota
No 18	Scampton	August 1953	Dakota
No 21	Scampton	September 1953	Mosquito VI
No 40	Coningsby	October 1953	York C 1
No 139	Hemswell	October 1953	Mosquito B 35
No 76	Wittering	December 1953	Dakota
No 58(PR)	Wyton	December 1953	Mosquito PR 35
No 82(PR)	Wyton	December 1953	Lancaster PR 1
No 90	Marham	January 1954	Washington B 1
No 199	Hemswell	January 1954	Lincoln B 2
No 115	Marham	February 1954	Washington B 1
No 35	Marham	February 1954	Washington B 1
No 207	Marham	March 1954	Washington B 1
No 100	Marham	April 1954	Lincoln B 2
No 69(PR)	Laarbruch	May 1954	Mosquito B 16
No 61	Wittering	July 1954	Washington B 1
No 102	Gütersloh	October 1954	Liberator VI/VIII
No 103	Gütersloh	December 1954	Lancaster B I/III
No 104	Gütersloh	March 1955	Liberator B VII(FE)
No 31(PR)	Laarbruch	May 1955	Devon C 1
No 80(PR)	Laarbruch	June 1955	Hornet F 3
No 213	Ahlhorn	July 1955	Vampire FB 9
No 542	Wyton	November 1955	Spitfire PR XIX
No 88	Wildenrath	January 1956	Sunderland GR 5
No 17(PR)	Wahn	June 1956	Beaufighter TT 10
No 59	Gütersloh	August 1956	York C 1
No 32	Akrotiri	January 1957	Venom FB 1
No 73	Akrotiri	March 1957	Venom FB 1
No 6	Akrotiri	July 1957	Venom FB 4
No 249	Akrotiri	August 1957	Venom FB 4
No 45	Changi	December 1957	Venom FB 1
No 39(PR)	Luqa	July 1958	Meteor NF 13

COLOUR PLATES

1
Canberra B 2 WD987 of No 12 Sqn, RAF Binbrook, 1952
Delivered on 29 March 1952, WD987 was one of four Canberras that undertook Operation *Round Trip* to South America in October 1952. It had previously established a point-to-point record between London Heathrow airport and Eastleigh, Nairobi, on 28 September 1952. Seen here with PRU cerulean blue on its undersurfaces to minimise high altitude conspicuousness, and with the Binbrook flash in gold, WD987 was the first Canberra to be finished in Medium Sea Grey/Light Sea Grey on the uppersurfaces. It subsequently served on No 231 OCU before being scrapped on 27 April 1964.

2
Canberra PR 3 WE144 of No 540 Sqn, RAF Benson, 1952
Delivered on 19 May 1953, WE144 served with Nos 540, 82, 58, 69 and 39 Sqns and No 231 OCU, before being struck off charge on 16 June 1972.

3
Canberra B 2 WJ569 of No 149 Sqn, RAF Gütersloh, 1954
Delivered on 5 May 1953, WJ569 initially served with No 59 Sqn before being transferred to No 149 Sqn – the jet is marked with the latter unit's fin crest of an interlaced horseshoe and a flash of lighting. WJ569 subsequently moved to No 231 OCU, before being broken up at Marshalls of Cambridge in May 1971.

4
Canberra B 6 WJ780 of No 109 Sqn, RAF Hemswell, 1955
WJ780 sports the yellow and black fin marking of No 109 Sqn. Note also the horizontal Blue Shadow aerial on the forward fuselage. WJ780 later served with Nos 139 and 249 Sqns, before being converted into a B 16 and moving to No 6 Sqn within the Akrotiri Strike Wing. It was then converted into a B 66 and sold to the Indian Air Force in 1969.

5
Canberra B 2 WJ625 of No 100 Sqn, RAF Wittering, 1955
Showing the Wittering Wing yellow and black chequerboard marking on its fin, this aircraft also boasts a green disc to denote its assignment to No 100 Sqn. Subsequently, WJ625 joined No 21 Sqn, before being passed on to No 231 OCU. Converted into a T 17 electronic warfare trainer for service with No 360 Sqn from Wyton, the veteran jet crashed into the sea shortly after taking off from Gibraltar on 3 August 1983. Sadly, all three aircrew were killed in this incident.

6
Canberra B 6 WH948 of No 101 Sqn, RAF Binbrook, 1956
WH948 sports the No 101 Sqn lion-in-the-battlements fin crest as well as Suez stripes. Subsequently assigned to No 12 Sqn, WH948 was converted into a B 15 and served with Nos 32, 249, 73 and 45 Sqns. It then became an E 15 (essentially a B 15 with an enhanced electronic fit) and was used by Nos 98 and 100 Sqns until it suffered a starboard engine fire during an air test on 15 August 1977 and crashed seven miles northwest of Coltishall. Both aircrew successfully ejected.

7
Canberra B 2 WD965 of No 10 Sqn, RAF Honington, 1957
Delivered on 4 February 1952, WD965 served with No 617 Sqn before joining No 10 Sqn at Honington – it is shown here with the latter base's white pheasant fin insignia. WD965 subsequently served with Nos 15 and 44 Sqns before being scrapped on 7 September 1970.

8
Canberra B 2 WK111 of No 32 Sqn, RAF Akrotiri, 1959
Seen here with the blue and white No 32 Sqn marking on its fin, WK111 later served with No 73 Sqn before being converted into a T 17 and joining No 360 Sqn. It was scrapped in November 1994.

9
Canberra B(I) 6 WT320 of No 213 Sqn, RAF Brüggen, 1960
WT320 served exclusively with No 213 Sqn after its delivery on 30 November 1955. Here, the jet sports the unit's hornet marking on its fin, WT320 was sold back to BAC on 9 December 1969 and broken up at Salmesbury in 1976.

10
Canberra B(I) 8 XH208 of No 3 Sqn, RAF Geilenkirchen, 1960
XH208 served with No 59 Sqn from 1957 to 1959, and then with the re-numbered No 3 Sqn. The Canberra is depicted here marked with the latter unit's distinctive cockatrice emblem on its fin. The jet also has a 1000-lb underwing bomb rack. XH208 was struck off charge on 13 August 1971 and became a decoy aircraft at Brüggen.

11
Canberra B(I) 8 WT365 of No 14 Sqn, RAF Wildenrath, 1962
WT365 joined No 88 Sqn in October 1956, staying when it was renumbered No 14 Sqn in December 1962. The unit's 'winged plate' badge on the nose is flanked by coloured strips of blue-diamonds-on-white pattern. When No 14 Sqn disbanded in June 1970, WT365 was transferred to No 16 Sqn at Laarbruch. It was declared 'Non-Effective' in April 1971 and scrapped in January 1972.

12
Canberra PR 7 WT527 of No 31 Sqn, RAF Laarbruch, 1968
WT527 joined No 80 Sqn in July 1955 before moving across to No 31 Sqn. Its 'Goldstar' badge, seen here on the jet's fin, is based on the Star of India, the emblem representing the squadron's claim to being the first military unit to fly in that country – a feature it achieved in late December 1915. WT527 was retired in March 1971, becoming a decoy aircraft at Laarbruch. It was scrapped in 1978.

13
Canberra PR 7 WH780 of No 81 Sqn, RAF Tengah, 1968
WH780 joined No 542 Sqn in May 1954, before moving to No 58 Sqn and then No 81 Sqn – the latter unit's fin crest of a dagger in front of a mullet adorns the fin of this aircraft. WH780 was transferred to the Fleet Air Arm in February 1971 to be converted into a T 22 for Fleet Requirements and Air Direction Unit duties. It was scrapped in 1995.

14
Canberra B 16 WJ776 of No 6 Sqn, RAF Akrotiri, 1968
After entering service as a B 6 with No 139 Sqn from September 1954, WJ776 was converted into a B 16 prior to joining No 6 Sqn (with its fin crest of a stylised eagle preying on a serpent). The jet remained on the Akrotiri Strike Wing until March 1969, when it was converted into a B 66 for India.

15
Canberra B 15 WH964 of No 249 Sqn, RAF Akrotiri, 1968
WH964 was delivered to No 12 Sqn as a B 2 in March 1955, and it was subsequently converted to B 15 standard. The Canberra then served with Nos 73, 32 and 249 Sqns within the Akrotiri Strike Wing, and it is depicted here with the latter unit's elephant fin crest and yellow spear on the wingtip tank. WH964 was eventually converted into an E 15 and flown by Nos 98 and 100 Sqns until retired in January 1982. Initially displayed at RAF Cosford, the jet was scrapped in September 1991. The nose section was preserved, however, in a private collection in Chailey, East Sussex.

16
Canberra B 16 WH959 of No 45 Sqn, RAF Tengah 1968
Delivered as a B 2 to No 12 Sqn in March 1955, WH959 was converted into a B 16 and joined No 45 Sqn – note the unit's winged camel crest on the fin. It was acquired by BAC in May 1969 and converted into a B 66 for India.

17
Canberra PR 7 WJ821 of No 58 Sqn, RAF Wyton, 1969
WJ821 was delivered in September 1954 to No 82 Sqn at Wyton when it converted from PR 3s. The aircraft moved across the airfield to No 58 Sqn when No 82 Sqn closed down in 1956, before being transferred to No 13 Sqn at Akrotiri, Luqa and then back to Wyton. Its starboard engine disintegrated on take-off on 25 July 1980 and the pilot made a force-landed at Bedford. Declared a Category 5 write-off, WJ821 performed the role of gate guardian at Bassingbourn Barracks from May 1981 until it was scrapped in 2013.

18
Canberra B 6(RC) WJ775 of No 51 Sqn, RAF Wyton, 1970
One of four modified B 6s fitted with Blue Shadow radar (note the 'wave guide' strake on the starboard fuselage side), this aircraft was initially delivered to No 192 Sqn at Watton. It was then passed on to No 51 Sqn after conversion to B 6(RC) configuration with British-designed Sigint sensors in an extended nose radome. The jet's Blue Shadow radar was used to fix its position before engaging in Sigint. WJ755 was retired to become a ground instructional airframe at the Central

Servicing Development Establishment at RAF Swanton Morley in 1974.

19
Canberra PR 9 XH174 of No 13 Sqn, RAF Luqa, 1972
Delivered in October 1960, XH174 served with Nos 58, 39 and 13 Sqns. The latter unit's tail crest, seen here on the fin of the Canberra, is a lynx's head – indicating vigilance – in front of a dagger. XH174 subsequently returned to No 39 (1 PRU) Sqn and was retired to St Athan in May 1989. Dismantled during 1991, only the aircraft's nose survives.

20
Canberra T 4 WT480 of No 231 OCU, RAF Cottesmore, 1972
This aircraft served with No 102 Sqn, No 231 OCU and Nos 7 and 360 Sqns, before returning to No 231 OCU. WT480 ended its RAF service with No 39 (1 PRU) Sqn. It is now privately owned in Ilshofen, Baden-Wurttemberg, Germany.

21
Canberra PR 9 XH168 of No 39 Sqn (1 PRU), RAF Wyton, 2003
Delivered in April 1960, XH168 served with Nos 58, 39 and 13 Sqns, before going back to No 39 (1 PRU) Sqn at Marham. Here, it is depicted sporting the *Eastern Promise* nose art and Scud-hunting mission markings from its service over Iraq in March-April 2003. After a landing accident in September 2003, XH168 became a source of spares for the remaining PR 9s prior to it being scrapped.

BIBLIOGRAPHY

Beamont, Roland and Reed, Arthur, *English Electric Canberra*, Ian Allan (1984)
Brookes, Andrew, *Photo Reconnaissance*, Ian Allan (1975)
Cull, Brian with David Nicolle and Shlomo Aloni, *Wings over Suez,* Grub Street (1996)
Delve, Ken, Green, Peter and Clemons, John, *English Electric Canberra*, Midland Counties Publications (1992)
Jefford C G, *The Flying Camels*, privately published (1995)
Jefford, C G, *RAF Squadrons*, Airlife (2001)
RAF Historical Society Journal, *The Canberra in the RAF* (2009)
RAF Historical Society Journal No 39 (2007)
RAF Historical Society Journal, *Royal Air Force in Germany 1945-1993* (1999)
Jackson, Robert, *Canberra – The Operational Record*, Airlife (1988)
Lee, Sir David, *Flight from the Middle East*, HMSO (1978)
Lee, Sir David, *Wings in the Sun*, HMSO (1989)
Taylor, Bill, *Royal Air Force Germany*, Midland Counties Publications (2003)
Wilkinson, Phil, 'Canberra Crusaders', *FlyPast*, Key Publishing (June and July 2005)
Wynn, Humphrey, *RAF Nuclear Deterrent Forces*, HMSO (1994)

INDEX